BEETHOVEN FOR A

Edward Dusinberre is first violinist of the world-renowned Takács Quartet. The Takács' recordings of Beethoven's string quartets, released on the Decca label and widely considered one of the most significant recent recordings of the repertoire, have earned numerous awards world-wide, including a Grammy, two Gramophone Awards, and BBC Music Magazine's 'CD of the Year'. They will perform complete cycles of the Beethoven quartets in the USA and London in the 2016/17 season. Dusinberre has also recorded Beethoven's last two violin sonatas for Decca, and is Artist-in-Residence at the University of Colorado Boulder.

Further praise for *Beethoven for a Later Age*:

'A richly detailed portrayal of the intimate workings of a great string quartet, in this case the magical Takács, as revealed to us through the recollections of its first violinist. Fascinating certainly to someone working in another artistic realm entirely.' Philip Roth

'Gathering up and reflecting on the work of his predecessors is not the least of Edward Dusinberre's achievements in a book unlike any other in its field, to be considered and enjoyed by anyone with more than a passing interest in Beethov

'This singular memoir looks both into the mind of a string quartet player and into the collective mind of his ensemble. It's a portrait not of science but of art: fluid, evolving, obsessed with the disciplined, elusive, ultimately impossible quest for something definitive, at the same time subject to the inspirations of the moment and the presence of the cougher in the second row. The book will be something between informative and revelatory to readers from musicians to music lovers.' Jan Swafford, author of *Beethoven: Anguish and Triumph*

BEETHOVEN FOR A LATER AGE

The Journey of a String Quartet

EDWARD DUSINBERRE

FABER & FABER

First published in 2016
by Faber & Faber Ltd
Bloomsbury House
74–77 Great Russell Street
London WC1B 3DA
First published in the US by The University of Chicago Press

This paperback edition published in 2016

Typeset by Faber & Faber Ltd
Printed and bound by CPI Group (UK) Ltd, Croydon CR0 4YY

A CIP record for this book
is available from the British Library

ISBN 978-0-571-31714-1

2 4 6 8 10 9 7 5 3 1

To Beth and Sam

Art demands of us that we do not stand still.

Ludwig van Beethoven, on the late quartets

They are not for you, but for a later age!

Ludwig van Beethoven, on the Opus 59 quartets

Members of the Takács Quartet

Gábor Takács-Nagy, first violinist, founding member,
1975–92

Károly Schranz, second violinist, founding member,
1975–present

Gábor Ormai, violist, founding member, 1975–94

András Fejér, cellist, founding member, 1975–present

Edward Dusinberre, first violinist, 1993–present

Roger Tapping, violist, 1995–2005

Geraldine Walther, violist, 2005–present

Contents

List of Musical Examples

Prologue

Opus 131

No sooner do I play my opening notes in Beethoven's late string quartet, Opus 131, than a man in the first row of London's Wigmore Hall coughs ominously. A teacher once suggested to me that coughing in an audience is inspired only by a boring performance. If that is so, this particular verdict has been reached swiftly. I wonder why the man doesn't escape from his seat. Perhaps he knows that there are no breaks between the seven movements of Opus 131 – if he gets up now the ushers may not allow him to re-enter the hall. Hopefully both boredom and phlegm will dissipate.

There shouldn't be anything especially taxing about the opening phrase of Opus 131; as first violinist of the Takács Quartet I have been playing Beethoven's fifteenth string quartet for nearly twenty years. I play the first twelve notes on my own:

The rhythm is uncomplicated, the tempo comfortably slow, but even the simplest-looking phrase is challenging: there are so many different ways one could play it. Over the last twenty years I have received copious suggestions from my dear colleagues in the quartet. First of all, how to play the *sforzando* (*sf* in the example above), an instruction to emphasise or attack a particular note?

That sounds too aggressive, could you try a more expressive version?

But now it sounds easy-going – not painful enough.

How about the tempo?

If it's so slow there's no sense of line. This is just the beginning of a long story.

But not so fluent that it seems easy-going.

Or the dynamic and type of sound?

Try playing it a bit quieter: inner grief, not explicit.

But not tentative or thin-sounding.

A Beethoven phrase can make seemingly contradictory musical demands. Dramatic yet understated. Slow but with a sense of direction. A private grief expressed in a hall to five hundred people. No wonder that this opening melody provokes debate: the choices I make affect my colleagues' options when they come to play the same phrase.

One after another they join me: Károly Schranz (Karcsi), the second violinist and one of two remaining original members of the quartet; Geraldine Walther, in her tenth year as our violist; and András Fejér, the quartet's cellist since its formation in Budapest in 1975. Unless there is some consistency in our approach to this melody, the audience will be confused as to the overall mood we are trying to convey. And yet Beethoven doesn't intend the four statements of the theme to sound identical. With each entrance the phrase descends in register, beginning in the middle range of the first violin, moving to the lowest string in the second violin, followed by the darker sound of the viola and finally the resounding bass tone of the cello: an intensifying of texture and emotion evolving from the first violin solo.

Even though we play the melody with the same basic

dynamic shape and tempo, each person plays it slightly differently: Karcsi's *sforzando* contains the most anguish; Geri's warm sound suggests both sadness and consolation; András' version is more understated, played with a leaner tone that brings out an introverted aspect to the melody. I can't judge what I bring to the mix: perhaps I should ask the bronchial gentleman in the front row. Although I am sorry that his concert is off to an unpromising start, a persistent cough is more distracting than a one-off event that can be easily dismissed onstage – a dropped programme or a snippet of commentary that projects more than the speaker realises: *Nice seats we have this evening.*

The combination of cooperation and individual expression that the opening of Opus 131 requires is central to the challenges and rewards of playing in a string quartet. Too many cooks may spoil the broth but in a quartet satisfying consensus can be achieved only when all four players contribute their zesty seasonings to the stew. I am fortunate for the last ten years to have shared this endeavour with Karcsi, Geri and András, always questioning and eager to find ways that we could improve our playing.

During the morning's rehearsal on the Wigmore stage, the inevitable debate about this opening melody focused on the question of tempo and how that influences the character of the music. Geri and I worried that we were playing ever more slowly, and as a result sounded 'notey', an unflattering term in our rehearsal vocabulary to describe the sense that each individual note is too significant – like a SENTENCE WHERE EVERY WORD IS SPOKEN WITH EQUAL EMPHASIS for no apparent reason. We were concerned about losing the audience's attention so early in the piece. But for András the worse crime was to play too fluently, to sound lightweight or impatient: Beethoven often begins a piece with a short slow introduction, but his daring choice to extend this idea into a whole movement should be embraced fully.

Karcsi stayed out of the fray, offering instead to listen from out in the hall. Escaping from the stage allowed him to judge our playing from the audience's perspective. We played a slower and faster version, trying to make each as convincing as we could. Karcsi would not be able to compare the options fairly if, during the slower version that András favoured, I played like a child being dragged along on a mandatory family excursion.

The prior discussion had already influenced our playing. Now Geri and I were keen to show that we could combine a faster tempo with enough gravitas, while András concentrated on moving as smoothly as possible from one note to the next, demonstrating that thinking in two beats per bar could still be accomplished at a slow pace.

'There's not much difference,' Karcsi reported. 'It's good if our bow speeds stay the same. If one person suddenly uses more bow we sound too restless.' In this case reminding each other of the different demands of this opening music had served to unify our approach.

When we return to a Beethoven quartet, continuing to argue over such basic questions of tempo and character, we can seem like a group discovering this music for the first time. A friend and board member of the Corcoran Gallery's chamber music series in Washington DC once invited us to rehearse in his living room. Having only ever heard us play in a concert, he looked stunned at the end of our rehearsal: 'Sometimes you guys sound like you have no idea what you're doing.' But even when we engage in a nerve-racking re-examination on the day of a concert, I relish a process that helps to maintain a sense of immediacy in music we have been performing for many years. A concert may benefit from many hours of preparation but the most exciting communication occurs when both audience and performers can suspend disbelief and discover the music afresh. The appearance of the ghost at the beginning of *Hamlet* would be less effective if, in a whispered aside, the actor reassured the audience that the confrontation had already been played out during an earlier matinee performance.

Our performance this evening of the first movement of Opus 131 benefits from the morning discussion. Geri enjoys drawing attention to a particular viola note; now András moves forward with more urgency than in our rehearsal. Knowing that the vibrant acoustics of the Wigmore Hall will project the smallest change of timbre or texture to the back of the hall, Karcsi experiments with a more transparent sound – I try to match him. In the first row the poor man continues his sporadic spluttering, less appreciative of the hall's acoustic properties.

Performing Opus 131 is always an adventure. Over the course of seven movements, played without a break, Beethoven covers an extreme range of emotions, shifting from one to the other with the minimum of preparation. However much we rehearse, I wonder how it will feel to play the fleeting, frenetic scherzo movement after an ethereal slow movement, or whether we will manage to create a big enough sound in the ferocious final movement.

Commenting to a friend on the startling originality of his late quartets, Beethoven explained, 'Art demands of us that we do not stand still.'[1] Beethoven composed his sixteen string quartets – seventeen if one counts the *Grosse Fuge*, which began its life as the last movement of Opus 130 but was later published separately as Opus 133 – at different stages of his life. They represent the most diverse body of work written in the genre by a single composer: the need we feel to revisit our interpretations is inspired in part by the spirit of exploration that runs through the quartets themselves.

Beethoven completed his first six quartets in October 1800, at the age of twenty-nine, and nearly eight years after he had moved from his birthplace of Bonn to Vienna. These first quartets, Opus 18, draw on the tradition of Haydn and Mozart's quartets but move in startling new directions. Between 1804 and 1806 he composed his next three string quartets, Opus 59, nicknamed the 'Razumovsky' quartets after the Russian count who commissioned them. The formal innovations and extraordinary range of expression of these later works shocked the first players and audiences who encountered them. Faced with trenchant criticism Beethoven retorted that they were music 'for a later age'.[2] Two more quartets followed, Opp. 74 and 95, in 1809 and 1810 respectively. Much later, in the three years before his death in 1827, Beethoven turned his attention predominantly to the string quartet, challenging the basic form of a quartet composition, reinventing the way in which the four parts relate to each other, and creating five masterpieces that daringly juxtapose the most sophisticated and sublime passages with music of childlike simplicity. No one has ever written a group of works that pose so many questions about the form and emotional content of a string quartet, and come up with so many different answers. In 1812 Beethoven described the fascination and curse of his vocation: 'The true artist has no pride. He sees unfortunately that art has no limits. He has a vague awareness of how far he is from reaching his goal.'[3]

Tackling the Beethoven quartets is a rite of passage that has shaped the Takács Quartet's work together for over forty years. From the earliest days these challenging pieces have been bound up with our evolution. The quartet was founded in Hungary in 1975 when Gábor Takács-Nagy, Károly Schranz, Gábor Ormai and András Fejér were students at the Franz Liszt Academy in Budapest. In 1979 they travelled to the first Portsmouth String Quartet Competition, which they won with a performance of Beethoven's Opus 59, no. 2, bringing them international attention. Four years later they were invited to the United States to study Beethoven's quartets with Dénes Koromzay, the original violist of the famous Hungarian String Quartet, who following his retirement from quartet playing taught at the University of Colorado. This visit began a life-changing association with the University of Colorado: in 1986 all four members of the Takács Quartet and their families defected from Hungary and settled in Boulder.

In the summer of 1993 I became the first non-Hungarian player in the ensemble, following the departure of its extraordinary founding first violinist, Gábor Takács-Nagy – an exciting and versatile musician, who now has a varied career as a conductor, violinist and teacher. During my audition for the quartet in 1993 I played the final movement from one of Beethoven's middle quartets, Opus 59, no. 3.

My arrival was the first of several changes. English violist Roger Tapping replaced original violist Gábor Ormai, who died of cancer in 1995. The last piece of music we played

7

with Gábor was the slow movement of Opus 59, no. 2 – the same piece that the Takács had performed in the finals of the Portsmouth competition, when the nineteen-year-old Roger Tapping was in the audience. With Roger we first played all the Beethoven quartets in six concerts at Middlebury College, Vermont, before further immersing ourselves in the music during further cycles in London, Paris and Sydney. We recorded the complete Beethoven quartets for the Decca label between 2001 and 2004, performing additional cycles during that period in New York, Aspen, Napa and Berkeley.

After Roger left the quartet to play and teach in Boston and spend more time with his family,* American-born violist, Geraldine Walther, for twenty-nine years principal violist of the San Francisco Symphony, joined us in 2005. She had first encountered the Beethoven quartets as a seventeen-year-old student at the Marlboro Music School and festival in Vermont, where each student ensemble was assigned an experienced chamber musician who both taught them and played in the group. Geri played her first late Beethoven quartet in the intimidating company of Sándor Végh – founding first violinist of the Hungarian and later of the Végh Quartet. In our new formation we reworked our interpretations of the Beethoven quartets, performing another Beethoven cycle at the South Bank Centre in London in 2009–10. In spring 2014 we turned our attention to Beethoven's transcendent Opus 132, completed after the composer's recovery from a life-threatening illness, performing it in several places including the Aspen Music Festival and the Edinburgh Festival.

* The quartet bug is hard to throw and after an eight-year break Roger is now the violist of the Juilliard Quartet.

As Beethoven predicted, his sixteen string quartets have come to be appreciated in a later age and can now offer a reassuring presence to those chamber music subscribers worried by lesser-known or more contemporary offerings. But I imagine Beethoven responding with amusement to a concert presenter who came backstage recently to complain about the sprightly march in one of the late quartets that rudely shatters the celestial mood of the previous slow movement: 'Why did he have to write that awful little piece? It ruins everything!' Her reaction connects the experience of listeners today with those first players and audiences who struggled with the quartets, reasserting the power of familiar music to disturb us even now.

During my first years as a quartet player I could easily understand the bemusement of those players and audiences who first encountered these quartets. Now I wonder if an attitude of shock and puzzlement, far from being merely the easily scorned reaction of a novice, is in fact integral to appreciating the spirit of the music. Absorbing myself in the circumstances that surrounded the composition of the Beethoven quartets, learning about the reactions and motivations of the patrons who commissioned this music and the audiences that heard them, has been a way for me to prevent the music ever becoming too comfortably familiar, to ensure that the spirit of challenge of these quartets is sustained every time we perform them.

The man in the front row has stopped coughing and I risk a grateful glance in his direction. I shouldn't allow myself to be distracted but the stage is small and the first row of seats is directly beneath it. As soon as the stage manager opens the door we seem to be walking out directly into the audience. Many people here tonight have been listening to the Takács Quartet since the group's emergence in the early 1980s: friends, relatives, and supporters who have in their different ways helped the quartet over the years and care as much about our welfare as they do about how we play. During the first minutes of any Wigmore concert I fight the worry that I might disappoint them in some way. In the Green Room after the concert when we appreciate their enthusiastic responses, we know that they will also hold back any strong criticisms for a later date, unlike one unfamiliar audience member who came into my dressing room several years ago in Aspen, Colorado: *You're a little loud for the second violinist when he has the second melody in the first movement, the scherzo seemed too fast, and in general the phrasing could breathe a bit more; the Beethoven wasn't your strongest piece tonight but I loved the concert – come back soon!* When I commented on not being accustomed to quite such frankness and attention to detail backstage, her face lit up. *I'm so glad you don't mind: most performers get quite upset with me.*

Although our next visit to Aspen found me testing the lock to my dressing room door, the goal of any performer should be to inspire such engaged listening. For while it is always our responsibility to capture and retain a listener's attention, the quality of listening in a hall can in turn profoundly influence a performance: we are more likely to linger over a beautiful change of harmony or the last wisps of sound at the end of a slow movement if the hall is silent than if a man is placing a sweater into a rustling plastic bag or – as occurred during another of our concerts – a woman sitting in the front row has just taken off her left shoe and is examining it intently under the stage lighting.

As we approach the end of the first movement of Opus 131 the others in the quartet seem fully absorbed by the music in front of them. Geri looks up at Karcsi, playing with exactly the same speed of bow to match her sound with his; András sways a little to his right as he takes over the melody from Karcsi. Fortunately we have reached a favourite moment of mine. The last two notes of this opening movement are the same pitch but an octave apart. The pause sign over the second note gives us the licence to hold on to it as long as we feel appropriate. Beethoven now repeats the same octave interval but up a semitone and forming the beginning of a tender, fleeting melody: with the minimum of preparation the character of the music is transformed.

Should the last note of the previous movement die away so that the first notes of the new tune enter with a new timbre of sound – a surprising change of direction? Or should we sustain our sound on the last slow note to make the join as smooth and continuous as possible, beginning the new melody with the same sound with which we finished the previous movement? Combining seemingly contradictory thoughts would be ideal: we want to convey the surprise of sudden change but maintain a sense of logical continuation.

During the morning rehearsal we talked mainly about playing the new melody with a livelier sound and tempo from the outset. But this evening, due in part to the attentive silence in the hall, we hold the preceding note longer than usual, drawing out our *diminuendo*. The next melody emerges with the same fragile sound, taking a few notes fully to establish the new faster tempo – this evening the change of character between the end of the first movement and the beginning of the second is less sudden than it sometimes is.

Balancing unity and contrast in our interpretation is again an issue in the fourth movement of Opus 131. This slow movement begins with a simple, serene melody supported by basic chords, allowing the maximum possibilities for development. In the following variations Beethoven transforms the theme, creating such a dizzying variety of rhythms, moods and textures that sometimes the story is as hard to follow as the boldest jazz improvisation. The most striking innovation comes toward the end of the movement. After each instrument is left on its own to play short, exploratory cadenzas, the music recedes almost to nothing before finding its way back to the opening theme, played now in the second violin and viola parts but surrounded by a radically different accompaniment: the first violin and cello imitate a piccolo flute and drum from a marching band, challenging the ethereal atmosphere that has pervaded much of the previous music – folk musicians interrupting a solemn gathering. How should the melody react to its irreverent accompaniment? This evening I like the way Karcsi and Geri's melody resists András' and my accompaniment, a nostalgic memory evoked despite the forward march of the cello rhythm, change and continuity existing side by side.

The ferocity of the seventh and final movement of Opus 131 bears no relation to anything that has preceded it. After so much delicate playing in the earlier movements, this finale with its driving rhythms and belligerent *fortissimi* now demands the power of a full string orchestra. Will we be able to summon up sufficient energy to help bring this massive piece to a stirring conclusion? Tonight I find the extremity exhilarating: finally I can throw myself fully into the drama, unconcerned by anything happening in the audience or the cluster of broken bow hairs that tickle my forehead – until one of them becomes trapped in my left hand and briefly pulls my bow off the string. Even this mishap adds a sense of intoxicating danger to this searing final transformation that seems to threaten the structure of the piece and the health of the performers. The risk of losing control lies at the heart of any vivid encounter with one of the later Beethoven quartets: music that at times consoles but also has the capacity to destabilise listeners and players alike.

Opus 131 ends in a surprising way. The first violin and viola play a descending melody, an exhausted answer to my opening gesture of the whole piece, while the second violin and cello's faster rhythm continues to agitate beneath the tune. The pleading melody seems to succeed in pacifying the underlying rhythm until from the bottom of the group András suddenly reintroduces the faster opening tempo and rhythm, leaping upwards through a C sharp major arpeggio. We all join in, ending the piece with three *fortissimo* major chords – a precipitous resolution.[4]

However much force we apply to the chords, they cannot fully resolve this immense piece and are greeted tonight, as so often, by a short, stunned silence. The way in which audiences react to this ending is different from the way they respond to Beethoven's middle works, such as the Fifth Symphony, where the repetition of final chords is so emphatic as to leave one in absolutely no doubt that the ending is upon us. The only question there is which of the many chords will prove to be the very final one – a feature parodied in Dudley Moore's magnificent Beethovenian presentation of the 'Colonel Bogey March'. But we are unlikely at the end of Opus 131 to hear an audience member exclaiming in delighted tones – as someone did immediately after the last note of another piece we played at the Wigmore – *That's it!* To create convincing finality in a piece so varied and which has moved continuously through its seven movements is perhaps an impossibility. Except for the small practical matter of physical exhaustion, the last three chords leave me wanting to go back right to my opening notes and start the journey again.

Of all the Beethoven quartets, Opus 131 is the most ambitious: how seven such contrasting movements manage to complement each other and be so convincingly bound together is a miracle no amount of musical analysis can explain. And yet my judgement of the piece as a satisfying unity is based on many years of experience living with the music; when I first encountered Opus 131 the extremity of its contrasts seemed daunting and irreconcilable. But through happy and despairing times the Beethoven quartets have accompanied the Takács Quartet. No wonder that music which itself grapples with the balance between unity and contrast, continuity and transformation, has been such a stalwart partner, helping us both to celebrate and to withstand change. Twenty-five years ago, when I was a student at the Juilliard School in New York, I had no idea of the ways in which these works could bind the lives of players and listeners together, music that itself emerged from a complex web of interactions between Beethoven, his patrons and the string players who first rehearsed these works.

We bow at the end of our performance and I have just enough time to put my violin in its case before we hear a knock at our Green Room door.

Audition: Opus 59, no. 3

Practice does not necessarily make perfect. Blundering my way repeatedly through difficult passages was not improving the first violin part of Beethoven's String Quartet, Opus 59, no. 3. In danger of forming an antagonistic relationship with the final movement I could hear the composer's derisive retort when Ignaz Schuppanzigh, the Viennese violinist most closely associated with Beethoven's quartets, complained about the difficulties of these latest quartets: 'Do you suppose I am thinking about your wretched fiddle when the spirit moves me?'[1]

This *Allegro molto* was one of several movements the members of the Takács Quartet had selected for my audition in January 1993. I wondered why a group that had already been playing concerts worldwide for eighteen years would consider hiring a twenty-four-year-old graduate student from the Juilliard School, with no prior professional string quartet experience. My teacher, Dorothy DeLay, had been asked by Fay Shwayder, a friend of the Takács Quartet, to recommend one of her students and explained that it was sometimes easier for a quartet to choose a malleable player fresh out of college than an established artist who might less easily adapt to the distinct musical personality of an ensemble, developed over many years.

My first audition with the Takács would take place in Boulder, Colorado, where the quartet had held a university residency since 1986. I guessed that the Takács had chosen

this particular Beethoven movement for its technical difficulties. The viola begins with a fast solo theme, taken up in
turn by the second violin and cello, the first violin last to
join the frenzy. I had never come across a Beethoven movement so unashamedly flashy, a virtuosic showpiece where
the challenge of playing the right notes seemed more press-
ing than any questions of musical interpretation. I could
move my left hand fingers and bowing arm fast enough,
just not at precisely the same time as each other. Hopefully
familiarity would facilitate greater velocity and more nim-
ble coordination. In the mean time Beethoven seemed to
mock my slow practice tempo, laughing at my violinistic
limitations and questioning my suitability to audition with
the Takács.

The first string players to encounter these pieces were
also challenged by them. Six years younger than Beethoven,
Ignaz Schuppanzigh began his musical education as a violist, changing to the violin only in 1793, at the age of sixteen.
Several years later Beethoven described Schuppanzigh as a
miserable egoist and would have enjoyed the joke: *Why
does a violin appear smaller than a viola? They're the same size
but the violinist's head is bigger.*

Throughout a professional association that lasted more
than thirty years, Beethoven sported a satirical attitude to
Schuppanzigh, nicknaming him after Shakespeare's Fal-
staff, not for the size of his head but for the rotundity of his
stomach: 'He might be grateful to me if my insults were to
make him slimmer.'[2] But his attitude was not always so
jovial. Writing to a close friend, Karl Amenda, Beethoven
described Schuppanzigh and the amateur cellist Nikolaus
Zsemskall 'merely as instruments on which to play when
I feel inclined'. These musicians 'can never be noble

witnesses to the fullest extent of my inward and outward activities, nor can they ever truly share my life. I value them merely for what they do for me.'[3]

As I continued to work on my audition music, Beethoven's objections about his musicians provided a useful jolt. Having spent many hours over the last three years labouring in a practice room while fretting about how to progress in the music profession, I recognised self-absorption as a not exactly elusive concept. But Beethoven's letter to Amenda was a more interesting subject with which to occupy myself than the question of my suitability as a candidate for the Takács Quartet, providing an intriguing snapshot of Beethoven's emotional state nearly a decade after he had moved to Vienna. While I couldn't enter fully into the 'inward and outward activities' of his life, any extra information would give me another angle from which to approach my audition music.

Beethoven moved from Bonn to Vienna in November 1792, at the age of twenty-one, to study with Europe's most celebrated composer, Joseph Haydn. His mother had died five years earlier and Beethoven ended his teenage years as the primary breadwinner for his alcoholic father and two younger brothers, relying mainly on his income as a court musician in the Electorate of Cologne, one of three hundred German-speaking states under the umbrella of the Habsburg or Holy Roman Empire, whose emperor resided in Vienna. Beethoven's precarious family situation played itself out against the backdrop of increasing instability in Europe: in April 1792, France declared war on the Habsburg Empire, and the rise to power of Napoleon in 1799 and the Napoleonic Wars would dominate European life for the next fifteen years.

Establishing himself during his first decade in Vienna as a pianist renowned for his expressive improvisations, Beethoven continued to develop as a young composer about whom his patron in Bonn, Count Waldstein, had made a prophecy: 'Through uninterrupted diligence you shall receive Mozart's spirit from Haydn's hands.'[4] (Mozart died in 1791.) A letter from Waldstein introduced Beethoven to a network of aristocratic patrons who helped to enable Beethoven's rise to prominence. But by 1801 Beethoven felt that his early successes were threatened by the deterioration of his hearing, as he confided to Amenda:

> In my present condition I must withdraw from everything; and my best years will rapidly pass away without my being able to achieve all that my talent and my strength have commanded me to do – Sad resignation, to which I am supposed to have recourse.[5]

Beethoven's sense of isolation was perhaps increased by his determination to protect his professional reputation by concealing his condition from musicians such as Schuppanzigh. In the 'Heiligenstadt Testament' of 1802, a document addressed but not sent to his brothers and discovered only after his death, Beethoven continued to worry that his credibility as a composer would be ruined if his deafness became known. As a result he felt he must live as a recluse, although sometimes yielding to his desire for companionship.

> But what a humiliation for me when someone standing beside me heard a flute in the distance and I heard nothing, or someone heard a shepherd singing and again I heard nothing. Such occurrences brought me near to despair; it would not have

taken much more for me to end my life – only my art held me back. Ah, it seemed impossible to me to leave this world until I had created all that I felt was within me.[6]

During the four years following the crisis that prompted the 'Heiligenstadt Testament', Beethoven composed the 'Eroica' Symphony, the 'Kreutzer' Sonata for violin and piano, the 'Waldstein' and 'Appassionata' piano sonatas, the Fourth Piano Concerto and the Violin Concerto. The Opus 59 string quartets, commissioned by Count Razumovsky, the Russian ambassador in Vienna, formed part of the extraordinary body of works that emerged from Beethoven's despair. As he worked on the quartet the Takács had asked me to prepare, Beethoven had written on a sketch leaf a startling declaration that marked a significant change of attitude: 'Let your deafness be no more a secret – even in art.'[7] Rather than the virtuosic showpiece I had taken it for, perhaps the finale celebrated his defiance against his condition. As I continued the painstaking work of learning the notes in a practice room, I wondered how playing it with the members of the Takács would illuminate the character of this deceptively complex music.

I could see no one resembling the urbane violist of the Takács Quartet pictured on a CD cover: leaning back in an armchair, viola resting on his lap, Gábor Ormai's photo exuded ease and confidence. In the baggage claim area at Denver's Stapleton Airport a pale-faced man with rowdy ginger hair wearing a shapeless brown anorak passed me several times before I thought to wave my violin case in his direction. He glanced at me and then away as if in search of a viable alternative.

'Are you Gábor?'

He tried to cover his surprise with a rapid grin. 'You're Ed! Sorry to miss you. We were expecting someone older.' The quietly assertive expression looking out from the CD cover had not prepared me for restless, darting eyes that were hard to engage. 'Welcome! It's not far to Boulder. Are you tired after your flight?'

The Takács spent six months of the year travelling – I was not about to admit fatigue after a three-hour journey. We walked to Gábor's car as he pointed out the Rocky Mountains on the horizon. He spoke softly, head pushed forward, diminishing his natural height. For someone accustomed to performing in front of large audiences, the violist was surprisingly unassuming.

On the way to Boulder, Gábor explained that we would first have dinner together, and play through the audition pieces only the following morning. In the position of the Takács members I would have wanted to read through the music right away: in the event that a candidate ruled himself out with bad finger coordination in a Beethoven movement, obligatory social interaction could be whittled down to a quick sandwich and token campus tour.

'Why do you like string quartets?' Gábor asked as we left the airport.

'I've never really thought about quartets as a career but I always enjoy playing chamber music. What about you?'

'Quartets are not as glamorous as solo playing, and sometimes you feel trapped. We are always so close: if one person is suffering then we all suffer. But together we can create something special – much more than I can make on my own.'

A better answer than mine. It should have occurred to

me that, since the members of a string quartet spend more time with each other than with their families, my personality as well as musicianship would be under close scrutiny. Anxious to highlight my suitability for group endeavour, I mentioned a successful spell on the school chess team. Gábor promised to show me the chess program on his new computer, while I wondered why I had chosen a game not renowned for its emphasis on teamwork.

'Why did you study at Juilliard?'

'For some time I've been aware of problems in my playing, especially with my bowing arm.' Perhaps I could improve my flailing attempts at conversation by being more forthcoming. 'I still have some work to do to change bow more smoothly and keep my arm relaxed. But DeLay has been very helpful.'

Gábor looked concerned. While frequent displays of modesty at school in England were an important strategy for survival – *Look at that stuck-up wanker with the violin case: who does he think he is?* – self-deprecation didn't appear to be a good ploy here.

'Well, there are always things to work on. Can I ask how old you are?'

'Twenty-four.'

'That's young. Dorothy didn't tell us that.'

I couldn't think of a response. As we drove over the crest of a hill Gábor pointed out Boulder, nestled against the foothills of the Rocky Mountains, roofs of the university campus rosy in the late afternoon sun. When Robert Fink, Dean of the College of Music, first drove the Takács to Boulder, he pulled off the road at this scenic outlook. 'Enjoy the view; that's part of your salary.'

Gábor's story about Dean Fink had piqued my curiosity

about the history of the quartet: perhaps at dinner I could limit the damage of my inept interview technique by asking the members of the Takács how they had ended up in Boulder, a change of environment from their native Hungary surely more dramatic than any a new first violinist would face by joining the quartet.

'You must be Ed!' As I entered the restaurant a man wearing a matching denim jacket, jeans and a furry hat jumped up from the table. Although clearly recognisable as the second violinist, Károly looked more mischievous than his photo. 'Schranz, Károly. Call me Karcsi or Charlie, whatever you like. What do you want to drink?'

'Ginger ale, please.'

'Are you sure? We'll find out everything about you anyway.'

András, the Takács' cellist, asked some of the same questions I had fielded earlier that afternoon. His wild curly brown hair and ruddy tan suggested a laid-back demeanour somewhat at odds with his formal use of English. He listened to my answers, alert eyes conveying curiosity mingled with scepticism.

'Gábor says you are young.'

'I am turning twenty-five in just a few months.'

'Dorothy did not tell us that.'

'But I'm an oldest child – we have to grow up faster.'

'Károly is an oldest child too.' András raised his eyebrows dubiously.

'Younger is good,' said Karcsi. 'More energy!'

I mentioned that the first violinist of the Tokyo Quartet, Peter Oundjian, also a student of Dorothy DeLay, was my age when he joined the ensemble. Asked by András about my professional chamber music experience, I described the handful of paid concerts my student quartet had performed while I was at the Royal College of Music in London before going to Juilliard. A highlight was our appearance at a Downing Street Christmas party hosted by the then British Prime Minister Margaret Thatcher – from my account of this illustrious engagement I omitted my fifteen-pound fee and the fact that she had criticised our choice of too slow and lugubrious a tempo in 'Ding Dong Merrily on High'.

Having swiftly exhausted the subject of my professional qualifications, I asked how the members of the Takács had come to settle in Boulder. In 1982 the Takács had participated in a masterclass for Hungarian television, run by the violist Dénes Koromzay, the only member of the Hungarian String Quartet to play in the group for its entire thirty-seven-year history. From 1962 to 1970 the ensemble had been in residence at the University of Colorado. Following his retirement from playing, Koromzay returned to Boulder in 1980 to teach. When Koromzay asked the Takács to recommend a student quartet to study with him in Boulder, the Takács put themselves forward instead. Although they were already developing an international concert career, the members of the quartet were eager to add to their repertoire – particularly the Beethoven quartets, some of which they had not yet studied. After several shorter residencies with Koromzay, the quartet applied for and were granted a long-term residency at the university. In 1986 the members of the Takács and their families moved from Budapest to Boulder.

It was an exhilarating but disorienting change, differences of culture and language confronting the members of the Takács and their families each day. At one of the quartet's first concerts in Boulder Karcsi limped on stage with a bandaged foot: not comprehending a DISMOUNT sign during a bike ride had resulted in a brief and painful encounter with a rock cluster. When the quartet embarked on a six-week tour, their families were left to get to grips with a bewildering array of regulations. Knowing that in order to register her car some sort of additional paperwork was required, András' wife Kati (accompanied by Karcsi's wife Mari and both sets of children), entered a neighbourhood fire station, asking some surprised firemen where the right place was to get an 'emotion test'.

Throughout dinner the Hungarians were keen to emphasise that although Boulder was so far from their roots, their adjustment to living in the community had been greatly eased by the generosity of a number of European immigrants, some of them Hungarian, who extended hospitality to the Takács just as they had to the Hungarian String Quartet during their earlier Boulder sojourn. Additionally, members of the string faculty welcomed them to the university community and helped to arrange their residency activities. My teacher's friend Fay Shwayder had financed a large part of their initial residency, facilitated by the support of Dean Fink.

Nonetheless the three Hungarians expressed mixed feelings about leaving Hungary, feeling homesick for friends and families left behind and appreciative of their special status in Budapest. The founding members of the Takács had received a rigorous musical education at the Franz Liszt Academy. Two lessons of individual instruction each week on the instrument were supplemented by chamber music coachings and a separate session on sonata repertoire. Classes in music history and theory and orchestral rehearsals completed their weekly musical activities. Obligatory political philosophy and Russian language courses imposed by the Communist regime were not taken terribly seriously. Required to explain the sources of Marxism during an oral exam, András had offered the succinct answer that 'Feuerbach had been raised by sucking on Hegel's breasts'. Ludwig Feuerbach was indeed, along with Marx, a great admirer of G. W. F. Hegel and although András' irreverent breastfeeding thesis was unappreciated by a stony-faced examiner, he was nonetheless given a pass grade.

Although the Dean of the Franz Liszt Academy facilitated a flexible schedule and a manager in Budapest helped the Takács during the early stages of their career, other aspects of life behind the Iron Curtain were challenging. Hungary was more lenient than other countries but travel visas were often granted only at the last minute and border-crossing encounters were sometimes stressful – on one occasion a soldier had tried to put a stamp on the back of Karcsi's violin.

Music students were generally exempt from the standard compulsory two-year military service, but Karcsi was not so lucky and was forced to participate in a new experimental one-month military training course for musicians. Every day the reluctant recruits ran laps, stumbled through muddy obstacle courses, and attended lectures about Communism. Relief for Karcsi came in the form of an ingrown toenail that became mysteriously more troublesome as the training continued. A sympathetic and probably bored army doctor offered to remove it. Karcsi's subsequent convalescence was dominated by table-football games in the army infirmary, interrupted only when an army ambulance came to transport him to those activities that would not unduly stress his recuperating foot. While a harried examiner tried to evaluate thirty students, Karcsi pretended to dismantle a gun, timing his triumphant raising of the 'reassembled' weapon to coincide with those conscientious students who had actually performed the task. His firing accuracy test was circumvented when the supervising officer, unable to bear the incompetent and menacing way Karcsi held the rifle, seized it from him and took the shots himself.

'They're good stories,' said András a little wearily, as he affixed me with a keen stare. 'But we are supposed to ask you most of the questions. How do you plan to balance your personal and professional life?'

I stuffed a spring roll into my mouth while the others looked at me, serious and awaiting my response.

'I've never really thought about that.' A common thread to my answers. 'I'm sure the quartet is so busy it would have to come first, at least until I know some repertoire. There can't be much time for a personal life.'

'You need someone to talk to,' said Gábor; 'we can be tough with each other.'

'Don't scare him,' said Karcsi. 'We're angels. But we need to fight sometimes.'

'How do you handle different musical opinions?' I asked.

'We get to play the same pieces many times so we can try lots of ideas,' said Gábor.

'The main thing is to agree on something and do the same thing; then the effect is much more powerful,' said András. 'We can always go back and change it tomorrow.'

'Agreeing can be hard,' said Gábor.

'Sometimes we nearly kill each other,' laughed Karcsi. 'That's string quartets.'

'We don't need to scare him,' said András. For the first time they spoke Hungarian.

'I'm sorry,' said Gábor. 'English is hard for us: too polite sometimes.'

Rehearsing in English would be a huge change for the others, but one to which they seemed resigned. András' wife was a language teacher and he hoped that perhaps the new player would take a few Hungarian lessons.

In this short time I was already getting a sense of how the others complemented each other: Karcsi, charismatic; András, responsible and measured; Gábor, sensitive, perhaps a mediator. How would a new player change the balance? Despite being grilled with questions at dinner, I was grateful that the first part of my audition had been social, emphasising how important relationships with quartet colleagues and with the larger community were to the life of a quartet musician.

Decorating the walls of the Takács Quartet's studio at the College of Music were posters from the Corcoran Gallery of Art's fine instrument collection, some of which were on loan to the Takács musicans. To my surprise Gábor sat opposite me, his three-hundred-year-old Nicolò Amati viola held far out to the left. I was accustomed to the viola being placed between the second violin and cello, but the others explained that with the cello in the middle they found the cello sound projected better, while the viola sound was more clearly defined when it was well separated from the violins. With the viola under his chin Gábor seemed to gain stature, reminding me of his confident CD cover photo. He looked around at his colleagues and smiled encouragingly before taking a brisk tempo in his opening solo of the Beethoven quartet movement. During cascades of quiet but lively quavers he maintained a calm posture, efficient arm movements making light of the technical challenges.

Beginning a movement with a ten-bar viola solo was a daring innovation – perhaps Schuppanzigh had briefly regretted his switch to the violin. Had the first violist to encounter the piece relished the exposure or reacted with disbelief, as my cousin had several weeks earlier during a read-through of my audition pieces with friends? *You must be joking: let's start where everyone else comes in.*

As with Gábor, I saw Karcsi and András in a different light when they began to play. Karcsi's impishness at dinner was now transformed into bustling energy as he entered with the same theme, leaning towards Gábor as they continued the *perpetuum mobile* together. Now András joined in, his quavers driving the group from the bass. What had seemed like an occasionally reserved, independent attitude at dinner was transformed into dogged determination – a strongly rhythmic cello line pulling the trio of Hungarians together.

Playing alone in a practice room, I could not have imagined the excitement the others would generate in the gradual *crescendo* that preceded my entrance: an ideal implementation of the dynamic increase that Beethoven had marked with red pencil in his manuscript score. As the *crescendo* culminated in a *forte* I joined in, swept along by the momentum. The first violin entrance seemed to encapsulate the potential demands on whoever would become the new Takács player, required to adjust instantly to a vital organism.

The rapidly changing function of the first violin part

now occupied me more than any technical challenges. After the three lower parts drummed out emphatic chords beneath my faster notes, Karcsi and Gábor took over my rhythm – a joyfully competitive answer. The argument escalated for two bars, the rhythm thrown to and fro between us before I set off on my own again, momentarily supported by accompanying chords but then spiralling downwards in a brief solo cadenza, a mix of dialogue and solo pyrotechnics.

First violin passages that had seemed to convey a serious character in my practice room were transformed by the music around me. Above one passage Beethoven gave the first violin the instruction: *sul una corda*. Played across three strings this first violin passage would have sounded light-weight and ordinary, whereas climbing higher and higher on the G string I had to dig in deeper with the bow to punch the notes out: the sound was earthier, and the increased difficulty added to the drama. Now I noticed the satirical nature of the accompaniment. Károly and Gábor bounced off András' beats, drawing attention to their flippant accompaniment by lifting their bows more than necessary after each note, seeming in their comic repetitive motion to mock the intensity of my part.

The roles shifted. Károly played the *sul una corda* effect while I joined the continuing 'oom-pah' accompaniment. Then it was Gábor's turn to climb up one string. Károly and Gábor seemed to relish the unusual assignment of moving their left hands further and further up their finger-boards, circus performers taking on an acrobatic challenge. When András executed the same effect on his cello his left hand moved away from him towards the floor, head bending so far over the instrument that he looked as if he might topple over. The physical demands of the music contributed to the drama.

Halfway through the movement the opening viola solo returned but this time accompanied by the first violin. Since I was playing the easier part with longer notes I was careful not to go too fast. Gábor stopped playing and said he felt held back by my rhythm – it would help his musical character if I could play on the front of each beat. When I played it as Gábor suggested the first violin rhythm added buoyancy to the viola solo. Again, musical character was the priority in a movement I initially thought had been assigned merely to test my technical ability.

Throughout the movement I was struck by how the body language and facial expressions of the Hungarians helped to convey the mood of the music. In their approach to musical character the Hungarians reminded me of my Ukrainian violin teacher at the Royal College of Music. Felix Andrievsky encouraged his students to communicate the emotional content of the music with every ounce of their beings. 'You're doing this only because I told you to but it must come from inside,' he would comment, an operatic personality who danced, sang and worked extreme facial transformations to get his points across. One midsummer evening I began to play Fritz Kreisler's 'Liebesleid' (Love's Sorrow) in my lesson. 'But Edwaaard,' he interrupted in his heavy accent, always drawing out my name when entreating me to play with more feeling, 'where's your sorrow?' He turned off the lights in his teaching studio. From the window I could see the illuminated red brick and majestic window arches of the Royal Albert Hall opposite as dim figures descending the steps below receded into the dusk. 'Now play again for someone you have lost.' Andrievsky could break through the sometimes inhibiting preoccupations of violin technique to get at the essence of a mood. Here again in the Takács Quartet studio, I felt notes prepared in a practice room come alive in the midst of these spirited musicians.

At the end of the Beethoven movement I asked if the tempo had been fast enough. Gábor provided the far from reassuring reply that it would probably go faster in concert. Like a married couple recounting differing versions of the same story, the Hungarians felt no need to offer a unified front: András said that he did not enjoy increases of tempo caused by concert adrenalin while Karcsi grinned and said it was fun sometimes playing at the edge of what was sensible. As seemed often to be the case Gábor took a diplomatic position, stressing the importance of spontaneity but in moderation.

When I asked the others about Beethoven's defiant declaration concerning his deafness written at the top of a sketch for this movement, Karcsi pointed out that the finale would make more sense in the context of the whole piece, particularly as an escape from a melancholy slow movement. This was the first time I had thought about the question of emotional balance in the piece: I wished I had had time to learn the other movements for my audition in order to understand better the function of this finale.

At the end of the session I mentioned to the others how much I enjoyed their discussions of musical character, even in this artificial audition setting.

'What else should we talk about?' Gábor laughed. 'If Dorothy sent you, we know you can play the violin, but in this short time we should try to find each other musically. It's good that you are enjoying thinking about it.'

*

'Why don't we have a look at the video before dinner?' András suggested. After lunch András had set up a camera onstage in the music hall before we played through several movements for the Takács' mentor, Dénes Kormozay. When comparing candidates it would help the others to have some evidence of our time together. Karcsi had explained that they would invite three finalists back to play concerts later in the spring: he should check with the others, he said, but so far I was top of his list. Grateful for his indiscretion I sank back into a sofa in András' basement, sipping on a second glass of Hungarian Bull's Blood wine.

As we walked onstage my visual incompatibility with the others was striking. The Hungarians wore the same combination of colourful shirts and jeans they had worn in the morning. My slightly short black trousers exposed white socks and faded blue suede shoes. A washed-out maroon shirt and overly long tie that dangled between my legs completed the ensemble: an awkward schoolboy tolerated by more sophisticated older brothers.

From the first notes the Hungarians inhabited the drama. As the music grew towards a climax, Gábor leaned in towards his music while András' head bobbed energetically from side to side. Karcsi's eyes darted to and fro, watching me to match a bow-stroke, and in the next moment catching Gábor's eye as they began to play a rhythm together. They made a dynamic unit, always alert to my and each other's musical intentions.

On the left side of the group, I communicated none of the exhilaration I had felt while playing, staring fixedly at my music as if it might at any moment vanish. With chest rammed upwards and chin clenched downwards onto the violin, I was like a shipwrecked sailor clinging to a piece of driftwood. It was a perplexing reminder of the difference between feeling and communicating emotion onstage. My inexperience was not translating into the agreeable malleability Dorothy DeLay had anticipated and I could hear Andrievsky's bemused plea: 'But Edwaaard, whaat are you doing?' After a few minutes I couldn't bear to look at it any longer.

'Can we stop this? It's bollocks.'

'What does that mean? Boll-ocks.'

'Rubbish, useless, a waste of time.'

'Bollocks,' András repeated with confidence. 'I like it: not so polite. Maybe we should rehearse more in English.' András turned off the video player. 'What don't you like in the playing?'

'You're all so natural looking. I seem to have a little box around me – I don't look part of the group. And the musical character doesn't come through.'

'That's great you can see something to work on. We often are discouraged after listening back to something. What could you do differently?'

'Pretty much everything. More flexible posture. More visual contact with you. I could smile once in a while.'

'That all comes with practice. Good that you're aware. And it's not as bad as you think: we've been playing together for eighteen years but already on the video we sound good with you!'

As we ate dinner with his family András seemed cheerful and more relaxed than at any time during my audition. I was discouraged: on the basis of the video surely I had failed the 'emotion test' part of the audition. The small amount of time I had spent playing with the three Hungarians had given me a sense of the richness and variety of their interplay, both as people and as musicians. After recent years spent focusing narrowly on improving my own playing, I would need to develop an array of collaborative skills to fit in with the Takács. And yet during the initial read-through I felt much more in common musically with the Hungarians than had come across in the video, enjoying their consistent attention to musical character which went hand in hand with a sense of fun and enquiry, surprising to me in a group so established. Whatever the outcome of the audition, it had provided a thrilling taste of collaborative music-making.

'How do you play this together?' I asked as we finished the slow introduction to Opus 59, no. 3. I had been invited back as a finalist to perform a concert with the Takács in April 1993. The concert would be one of the annual series of concerts that the quartet performed in Grusin Hall at the College of Music in Boulder. We had only three days to prepare a programme of quartets by Mozart, Brahms and Beethoven.

The first *forte* chord raises a question: what key were we in? The four notes of this chord make up a diminished seventh – diminished because while most chords are built upon a mixture of smaller and larger intervals, the diminished seventh consists of three minor thirds, piled on top of each other. The chord is dissonant, in need of resolution, functioning like a crossroads from which a number of different destinations can be reached. Such a moment might reasonably occur after the key and primary musical themes have been established, but Beethoven dares to disorient the audience from the very first chord of the piece. After a silence the next chord includes the same notes in the three upper parts while the cello line moves down a note – a quieter, *pianissimo* dynamic increases the uncertainty. The cello continues to creep lower before another loud diminished-seventh chord interrupts, re-emphasising instability. The bass line descends still further as the first violin climbs higher, disembodied and directionless.

We sounded aimless for the wrong reason: with so little in the way of rhythm it was hard to play with the same pulse as each other. Karcsi suggested that I lead the chord changes more clearly. I raised my violin a little in advance in order to give an emphatic downward gesture on each chord but the resulting improvement in ensemble came at the expense of character . . . now we sounded merely confident instead of exploratory. Despite repeating the opening section several times, we still struggled to feel the pulse together. The challenge was to convey that the music was in search of a path, not the musicians.

'Let's come back to it tomorrow,' said Gábor. 'Sometimes with a difficult passage we just have to take the vitamins each day.' Daily vitamin dosage was a concept perhaps more reassuring to musicians accustomed to a continuous cycle of rehearsals and concerts than a candidate with only three days to prepare for the most important concert of his life.

The robust rhythm and momentum of the *Allegro vivace* that followed came as a relief. Mindful of my stiff performance at the first audition, I looked around the group trying to glean pointers about how better to communicate character. Compared with other professional string quartets the Takács liked to sit quite far apart. The result was that neither second violin nor cello, sitting on the inside, were covered from view by the first violin and viola. Perhaps the extra space encouraged each player to develop a unique physical approach to his instrument. Karcsi's bowing arm was lively, with his flexible fingers and energetic forearm motion creating a vivid, dancing character. The freedom in his arms originated in his lower back: at times he seemed on the verge of jumping out of his chair. András leaned into his cello, arms surrounding it in an embrace. Gábor had the most upright posture, rotating from his hips to his left whenever he had a solo in order to point the viola and his sound towards the audience, then swinging the instrument back to play an accompanying figure with Karcsi.

An additional advantage of sitting in a wide arc, Karcsi explained, was that seeing my face instead of just my profile could give him more clues as to the mood I wanted to convey in the music at any moment. For the uninitiated, however, looking around the group while trying to play with a less rigid posture was a perilous activity. Unaccustomed motion led to my bow losing its contact point on the string, while establishing eye contact with Gábor as we played the same rhythm caused me briefly to lose my place in the music. The concise adage of a violinist friend came to mind – *Look up: screw up*. But in order to come closer to matching the open, uninhibited style of the Hungarians I would have to risk incorporating new ideas, however distracting. 'Playing it safe' didn't seem to form any part of the Takács' musical philosophy.

Sometimes a sense of danger came from not entirely resolving a difference of musical opinion. Two-thirds of the way through the first movement a dramatic *fortissimo* climax required both teamwork and a sense of opposition. Sharing a two-note figure, the viola and cello should play with exactly the same timing and emphasis before the two violins answered back with the same rhythm.

'András, your first note is too loud – it's just an upbeat: the second note should be stronger in each group.' Gábor played to demonstrate his point.

'I don't like the first note so light. This is a climax, everything should be *fortissimo*.' András sang his part, waving his arms to show the equal weight on each note.

'Your upbeat sounds louder than the arrival,' Gábor said.

Karcsi laughed. 'We always argue about this bit. The good thing about playing a piece many times is that we can try different ways.'

'Tomorrow let's try it my way,' said András, smiling.

Perhaps because Gábor and András had not agreed on exactly how to play the dynamic shape, both now played with greater energy, while tacitly modifying their ideas to get a little closer to one another's approach. To match their intensity Karcsi and I had to play louder and with more bite: now the dramatic opposition between the two pairs came through.

While the first-movement climax allowed for disagreement to be channelled into the musical drama, the opening of the third movement, a *Menuetto*, brought a different question of character to the fore. If the mysterious slow music at the beginning of the whole piece owed a debt to the opening bars of an earlier quartet in the same key by Mozart, which had earned it the nickname the 'Dissonance' Quartet, here in the opening phrase of the *Menuetto*, the music seemed again to recall Mozart. Beethoven's instruction *grazioso* required the character of an elegant, stately dance. We all began with a long note that developed into a faster semiquaver rhythm at the end of the bar. But my sound stuck out from the others' and the fast rhythm was restless, a nervous tic invading a serene face.

String players can vary the sound in a number of ways. By moving the bow further from the wooden bridge that holds the strings above the body of the violin, I made a more mellow tone, increasing the wispier quality by also playing with a faster bow speed. I could further affect the character of the sound by varying my use of vibrato – the degree of width and speed with which a left-hand finger oscillates below and back to the pitch. I tried to imitate the narrow vibrato of the others: now our matched sounds communicated the fragile sweetness of the tune. In the faster semiquavers I tried to spread the rhythm out more and played with as smooth a finger motion as possible – sudden motion would convey the wrong character.

In contrast the rambunctious Trio required short, incisive bow-strokes executed close to the bridge, a new character displacing the nostalgic lyricism of the opening section. My sound however was too crunchy. I tried to imitate Karcsi and Gábor's flexible right-hand fingers which functioned like shock absorbers, allowing the energy from their arms to be nimbly applied to each string.

Although there was more discussion during my second audition about the nuts and bolts of quartet playing – how to play together and in tune with each other – the Hungarians never lost sight of these issues as being a means by which to communicate emotion. When I first imagined what it might be like to work in the Takács Quartet, I was intoxicated by the promise of international travel and opportunities to play in the world's best chamber music halls. During my short time rehearsing with the group I began to realise that the fundamental work of the quartet took place here in this small studio where musical details of interpretation were hashed out. After three days of rehearsals I couldn't wait to play the concert: hopefully the additional time spent together would help me to seem more integrated into the group than I had done at my first audition.

Nothing seemed quite as it had in the stage rehearsal. Three hundred and fifty audience members dampened the acoustic so that the tone of my violin seemed to carry only an arm's length away. Blending sounds was difficult; each instrument sounded separately on the stage as if in its own acoustical box. Too aware that the audience were evaluating the Takács in this experimental formation, I judged everything I played: a bit flat on that note; not together with András; now a scratchy sound – the result of my bow sliding too close to the bridge. Making progress in rehearsal required constant evaluation but in concert I needed to find a way to turn off the self-critical commentary.

Now the pacing and dynamics came out slightly differently from how we had rehearsed them. The Hungarians drew attention to the unusual markings in the score: off-beat *sforzandi* were played with more bite; notes marked *tenuto* (sustained) were leant into as if treacle held the musicians' bows to the strings. A passage where each performer played a flurry of semiquavers became a vivid conversation, as Gábor threw his notes in the direction of Karcsi who in turn fixed András with a slightly menacing grin, speeding up a little as if daring András to respond in kind. I tried dropping to a softer dynamic in one phrase in order to make a more dramatic *crescendo*. Instantly the others adopted the same approach. An aspect of a performance with the Takács seemed to be *not* to do things exactly as rehearsed, the prior work providing a framework within which one could experiment in concert. Sometimes the most satisfying interplay involved contrast rather than strict imitation. When I played a figure more insistently Karcsi responded with a casual, lighter answer, cheekily questioning my character. I had approached my first audition video like a diligently prepared student who during an exam clings too rigidly to prepared answers, unable to react nimbly to unanticipated questions. Now I enjoyed more the element of spontaneity inherent in playing with three such lively and inventive musicians.

Performing Opus 59, no. 3 for an audience helped to define the character of the music onstage. During rehearsals the mood that András imagined in the slow movement had eluded me. The *Andante con moto quasi allegretto* is dominated by a simple scale-like theme that is repeated many times, often underpinned by quiet but relentless pizzicati (plucked notes) in the cello. András thought I sounded too expressive, instead of allowing a bleaker mood to emerge. If our audience during the concert had been restless and noisy, perhaps a more extrovert expression of grief would have seemed necessary, but now the silence in the hall encouraged us to play for each other, trusting that we could hold the listeners' attention with a more introverted character.

Beethoven's dramatic balancing of emotions between the movements was particularly effective in this performance situation. The repetitive melancholy of the slow movement, a sad thought returning with quiet insistence, was more effective after the emphatically cheerful first movement, seeming to recall the mysterious and wandering introduction. In the middle of the third movement the jocose Trio interrupted the graceful Minuet with delightful rudeness. A darkening of mood at the end of the movement created suspense, resolved only by the ebullient *Allegro molto*; drama, humour and virtuosity trumped all the previous characters in the music.

After so much interchange between the parts it was exhilarating when the four parts came together with bustling quavers at the end of the piece. Karcsi and Gábor joined me to climb higher and higher – instead of alone as in the *sul una corda* passage – while András cascaded down to the lowest note on his instrument. We all rocketed through the notes of a C major arpeggio and ended with two ferocious chords.

While the audience's enthusiastic applause might have been in part an encouraging vote of confidence in my playing, I would later realise that even a less than brilliant performance of this extraordinarily effective finale can inspire such a reaction. The technical and musical demands of Opus 59, no. 3 made it a suitable choice to test a first violinist, but there were additional reasons that made it a canny selection. Changing a player in a string quartet is a trauma that must be played out under the watchful eye of an expectant public as a group first selects finalists and then tries to assimilate the new player. The vivid emotional landscape and exhilarating conclusion of Beethoven's defiant response to personal suffering proved to be stalwart companions both for the seasoned members of the Takács and their inexperienced applicant.

This second audition had given me a snapshot of the Takács Quartet's way of life in Boulder – their routine of practising individually in the mornings before convening in the afternoon for a rehearsal of between four and five hours. Up to now I had viewed a concert as the end product of many hours' work, after which I would move on to study a new piece. But the constant debates in the Takács about phrasing, tempo and character altered my sense of the relationship between rehearsals and concerts, both now seeming part of an ongoing exploration of the music. Even as we performed the Beethoven quartet, I wondered how this concert experience might influence interpretative choices in subsequent rehearsals.

Before Gábor drove me back to the airport the day after the concert, he proudly pulled out his latest acquisition from the back of his car. It was a black-and-white etching that he had discovered at a garage sale, showing the members of the Alban Berg Quartet seated in playing positions.

'The owner was offering it for fifty cents. But come on, I argued, who plays classical string quartets nowadays? I got it for a quarter!'

My time in Boulder made me hope that I would be given the chance to become one of those lucky few quartet players, to have the opportunity of exploring the quartet repertoire with such engaging musicians. In particular, my audition had piqued my curiosity about the quartets of Beethoven, the circumstances under which they had been written, and how their creation had helped shape the careers of those musicians like violinist Ignaz Schuppanzigh who had first performed them.

Three months later Karcsi, Gábor and András phoned me in my New York apartment to invite me to join the Takács Quartet. András reminded me that during my first audition I had told them how excited I was to apply for the 'first violin job'.

'This is not a job: it's your family, your life. We hope you'll be with us for at least fifteen to twenty years.'

My dizzy exhilaration at the news was tempered only by the sense of how much work lay ahead of me to justify the brave risk the others had taken in choosing such a young musician to join them. I was anxious to return to the Takács rehearsal studio in Boulder as soon as possible and begin my new life as their first violinist.

2

Joining the Quartet: Opus 18, no. 1

We played the phrase one at a time, striving for the same timbre of sound, articulation and volume. This was a challenge: ask four people to recite a line of poetry and each will emphasise certain words more than others, varying the tone and volume of their voices. By repeating this process while listening and reacting to one another in the opening statement of Beethoven's first Opus 18 quartet we hoped to unify our musical and technical approach.

After one round Karcsi stopped.

A fenébe . . . jó lenne, ha hallgatnánk egymást!
Ne nézzetek teljesen hülyének!

'Sorry about the Hungarian. Sometimes English is too hard,' said Gábor. I had taken several Hungarian lessons with András' wife Kati but was an undisciplined student, effortlessly memorising swear words gleaned from my colleagues, absorbing irrelevant expressions from a phrase book – *terhes vagyok* (I am pregnant) – but unable to grasp basic grammar.

I had been living in Boulder for one month and we were at the beginning of our usual four-hour afternoon rehearsal. From the way Karcsi demonstrated on his violin, I didn't need to understand Hungarian to know that my colleagues were debating how to begin the first note, either with a positive consonant or something more softly stated.

'Try starting with an up-bow.' András played his part:

'The first note isn't so heavy and then we'll be in a better part of the bow to bite with the short notes.' Organising our bows to move in the same direction would create visual unity. More importantly, discussing bowing options would clarify how we wanted to shape the phrase.

A bow influences the character and type of sound to such an extent that some string players own as many bows as golf players do clubs. Each bow has its own unique balance of weight, strength and flexibility. String players often select different bows for different pieces of music, and find that a particular bow handles better in a dry or humid climate.

The most weight is at the bottom of the bow, or the frog, where the bow is held. Beginning the first phrase of Opus 18, no. 1 on a down-bow would facilitate stronger emphasis. Starting with an up-bow at the tip of the bow where the bow is lightest would make the beginning of the note more buoyant.

'It'll be harder to start an up-bow together,' I said, not yet observing a rule of good rehearsing technique: when someone has an idea it's better just to try it out instead of anticipating its disadvantages.

'I'm not sure about the down; then we're in a difficult part of the bow for the short notes,' said Gábor.

'I agree with Ed,' said Karcsi. András raised his eyebrows, a frequent means of expressing scepticism or mock surprise, in this case employed to register that Karcsi had yet again supported my point of view. Although he did not invariably back me up, Karcsi saw it as one of his primary roles to make life as easy for the first violinist as possible. He bore the brunt of the administrative work, talking to our managers daily as they planned our future concert schedule, leaving me time to practise all the new repertoire.

Given my inexperience I was astonished that during my first weeks in Boulder all three Hungarians spoke to me about the different aspects of leadership they expected from me: to structure the rehearsals so that we covered the necessary repertoire, to know when to move on a rehearsal conversation if we were getting bogged down in a given passage, and to come to rehearsal with plenty of musical ideas. Their approach seemed designed to help me not feel intimidated by their eighteen years of prior quartet experience.

After several minutes we still couldn't agree on which bowing we liked. Gábor suggested that I listen from the corner of the room with my eyes shut to see which version sounded better. There wasn't much to choose between the two bowings but I thought I could recognise the up-bow start with its airier sound, the first note blossoming in tone so that the short notes seemed to come logically from the energy of the first stroke. By contrast, the down-bow Karcsi and I had advocated sounded clunky and angular. We conceded the point. With the agreed bowing in place the opening phrase sounded more unified.

Being on the losing side of such an argument was at least compensated for by the opportunity to build up credit for future disagreements. I sometimes also resorted to the short-term strategy of introducing a controversial bowing ten minutes before the end of a rehearsal, acquiescence more readily achieved as stomachs rumbled in anticipation of chicken paprikás. Too easy consensus was unfortunately usually re-examined on full stomachs the following day.

Agreeing on the bowings, phrasing and character necessary to unify a phrase was only one element in the process of becoming first violinist of the Takács. During a summer festival concert I attended in Boulder shortly after moving there, I overheard two audience members talking.

'He's not nearly passionate enough. Gábor Takács was so spontaneous. This new one's not Hungarian – from England I think.'

'Ah well then,' the other replied, staring morosely into her programme booklet.

For eighteen years Gábor Takács-Nagy was a dynamic leader of the ensemble, playing with an expressive sound and edge-of-your-seat excitement: audiences would expect the same from me. But how to achieve these elusive qualities? Would my colleagues provide enough continuity to assuage the disappointments of those audience members who missed Gábor Takács' engaging presence? Despite the others encouraging me to assert myself in rehearsal, matching bow-stroke and phrase shapes seemed easier than the more nebulous question of how to project my own personality within the group. Strong leadership was required, but at the same time András valued flexibility: from my willingness at the audition to be self-critical he had seen the potential to modify more extreme musical ideas. If Karcsi and I pushed too quickly ahead in this opening movement of Opus 18, no. 1, András provided subtle rhythmic resistance – an aspect of a cellist's role was to counterbalance the occasional excesses of over-enthusiastic violinists. The question of how to be both more individual and more integrated into the ensemble would occupy me throughout much of my first five years as a quartet player. I hoped that Beethoven's first Opus 18 quartet – the second in order of composition but so successful that Beethoven adopted Ignaz Schuppanzigh's suggestion of publishing it as the first – would provide opportunities to explore individual expression, teamwork and the delicate relationship between the two.

*

The German writer and traveller Baron Johannes Kaspar Riesbeck, writing about Vienna some ten years before Beethoven moved there from Bonn to study composition with Joseph Haydn in 1792, observed a thriving musical scene and an impressive unity of execution in the private orchestras employed by some of the Viennese nobility:

> I have heard thirty or forty instruments play together, all of which gave so just, so clear, and so precise a sound, that you would have thought you heard only a single very strong instrument; a single stroke gave life to all the violins, and a single breath to all the wind instruments.[1]

Riesbeck however delivered a scathing verdict on what he viewed as rampant hedonism amongst Vienna's citizens. In coffee-houses or beer-houses where 'they breakfast till they dine, and they dine till they sup, with only the interval of, perhaps, a short walk and going to the play', the disparaging Baron observed 'nothing but a perpetual motion of jaws'.[2] Riesbeck was disappointed at the degree of political apathy he witnessed: 'You meet numberless people of the middling ranks who have nothing to say of their ministers, their generals, and their philosophers, and hardly know even their names.' Perhaps those of middling rank were only too glad to chew continuously on their cutlets, thus avoiding conversation with this sour dignitary.

When the English traveller John Owen visited Vienna a decade later and shortly before Beethoven's arrival in the city, he saw no signs of the apathy Baron Riesbeck had observed:

A principal part of my amusement arose from the warm debates of some worthy citizens, who, having dispatched the
business of the day, were relaxing their minds with a little
politics. I was diverted to hear these great personages regulat-
ing the affairs of empires – leading the combined armies into
the heart of France, by a shorter cut than the Duke of Bruns-
wick had taken – making the rebels own their lawful king,
and receive their expatriated princes.[3]

As John Owen prepared to leave Vienna on 5 November
1792, conversations were dominated by one subject:
'Whether I may experience any, or what interruption from
the progress of the French arms, I am little anxious to
know; but their extraordinary successes along the Rhine,
have filled the coffee-houses with clamour and predic-
tions.'[4] One day later, while the twenty-two-year-old
Beethoven was travelling from Bonn to Vienna, the French
army defeated the Austrian forces at the battle of Jemappes
(now in south-west Belgium) and captured the territory of
the Austrian Netherlands.

While Beethoven found lodgings and commenced his
first composition lessons with Haydn, he began to find his
place in a changing environment for musicians. The number of those private bands (*Hauskapellen*) financed by the
nobility and admired by Baron Riesbeck was decreasing, a
development caused at least as much by the petering out of
a fashion as by economic factors.[5] Between 1761 and 1790
Haydn had been in the service of the rich and powerful
Esterházy family, members of the Hungarian nobility and
committed patrons of the arts. From 1766 Haydn assumed
the position of *Kapellmeister* (music director) of the Esterházy court but in 1790, following the death of his employer,

Prince Nikolaus, the court orchestra was dissolved. Haydn took up residence in Vienna where he embarked on a freelance career as Europe's most celebrated composer.

With fewer opportunities to be servants of the nobility in private orchestras, musicians could assume a more precarious but potentially elevated status. Beethoven had himself been employed as a violist and organist in the Elector's court orchestra in Bonn, but now sought to establish his reputation as a pianist and composer in Vienna. Aristocratic patronage would however continue to exert a significant influence on the Viennese music scene throughout the course of Beethoven's life, manifested in a number of different ways. Thanks in part to a letter of introduction from his patron in Bonn, Count Waldstein, the young musician met several Viennese nobles during his first months in Vienna, including the man who would become one of his most influential supporters and friends.

A member of the same Masonic Lodge as Mozart, Prince Karl Lichnowsky (1761–1814) grew up in Vienna and later inherited a family estate near Troppau (now Opava in the Czech Republic). In 1788 he married Maria Christiane, the daughter of Countess Maria Wilhelmine of Thun-Hohenstein, herself an enthusiastic supporter of the arts in Vienna. The prince took piano lessons from Mozart and in 1789 organised a promotional concert tour for Mozart to Prague, Dresden, Leipzig and Berlin. Mozart did not find Lichnowsky to be an entirely reliable supporter – in Leipzig he reported needing to lend Lichnowsky some money[6] – and subsequently financial relations between the two soured. In 1791 Lichnowsky won a legal claim against Mozart for non-payment of a debt. The fact that Lichnowsky felt the need to pursue the debt was perhaps an indication of an aristocrat living beyond his means, a phenomenon commented on by Baron Riesbeck: 'Though most of the richest people have been for years oppressed by debts, they have not yet learned to confine their expenses, and would think it a shame to live within bounds.'[7]

But however flimsy the foundations for their opulent lifestyles, Lichnowsky and others would provide invaluable support for Beethoven during his first years in Vienna by commissioning new works, and offering rehearsal and performance opportunities in their homes. Out of this environment would emerge Beethoven's first chamber works. The unity of execution, so admired in the private orchestras by Riesbeck, would become one of the goals of the smaller chamber ensembles promoted by Lichnowsky and his friends.

'The pulse changes too much . . . too loud . . . sounds like chaos there!'

Professor Dénes Koromzay and I were listening to a recording of the Takács Quartet playing Beethoven's first Opus 18 quartet from a house concert in September 1993. Until now I had spent time with the ex-violist of the Hungarian Quartet only at dinner parties, where an atmosphere of good cheer surrounded this distinguished musician who had generously taken the Takács under his wing and helped them move to Boulder.

'Let's hear our interpretation.' Koromzay pulled himself out of the sofa, stooped over the record player and lowered the needle with a jarring crunch before the Hungarian Quartet's crisp opening phrase resounded through the room.

'You see,' Koromzay said, 'we're quieter and exactly together. That's easier at this slower speed. We worked hard on all the Beethovens during the Second World War while trapped in Amsterdam. By 1945 we had a large repertoire and started our career, playing the whole cycle.'

Koromzay moved back to the sofa, using a coffee table for support, and sat down heavily. For thirty-five years his days had been packed with intense rehearsals, travel, concerts, post-concert dinners and the daily drug of applause. Now the recently widowed violist relived his exhilarating life as a touring musician through his recordings. He listened to his old quartet, nodding occasionally to register approval.

'A steady tempo. It's hard to play this way when you are young. Borrow our record; just make sure to return it.'

'I don't own a record player,' I said, pretending to read my miniature score and wondering at my inability to receive criticisms more graciously. Although our playing was rough by comparison with the Hungarian Quartet's rendition, I wanted to defend the faster tempo that created a sense of restlessness and urgency arguably more in keeping with the spirit of a questing composer at the start of his career.

We had reached the end of the first exposition section during which the main themes of the music were laid out. After the first violin played a passage of descending semiquavers, the three other parts joined in with the same rhythm and notes to mark the end of the section – individuality giving way to the greater impact of all four musicians playing together, as at the opening of the piece.

'If you play too fast there, your colleagues can't easily join in with you: our version is stronger.'

Doubts about establishing myself as a professional

quartet player made me less receptive to Koromzay's feedback. When Karcsi had first sent me the list of approximately sixty concert engagements that made up our first
season, I had been thrilled at the opportunity to play in
some of the oldest chamber music series in Spain, Ireland,
England and Holland, and to end the season with a month-
long tour to Australia and New Zealand. But the concert
promoters who had booked the quartet as much as two
years previously had not expected that they would be listening to a new first violinist. Until such presenters were
convinced of my suitability I would feel like a pretender.

Even so I should say something appreciative about the
Hungarian Quartet's recording: the ensemble was one of
the important string quartets of the twentieth century and
formed a particularly close relationship with Béla Bartók,
whose six string quartets are some of the greatest works for
the medium in the first half of the twentieth century. It was
generous of Koromzay to share his knowledge with me.

'Thanks for playing it for me . . . but I have to go to
rehearsal now.'

'So soon? You should come more often and stay longer.
Gábor Takács was here most days. A great violinist and
musician, like a son to Suzy and myself.'

Koromzay shook his head and frowned as his old quartet continued to play. 'That doesn't sound clearly – there
should be more viola there. You see, it's never perfect.
Maybe we're too slow as well.' His lingering frustration
was surprising: many years later Koromzay was still trying
to modify his group's interpretation. I did not notice the
viola balance problem that he complained of; the Hungarian Quartet's performance seemed to capture an ideal mixture of control and excitement as the crackling dialogue of

four independent voices culminated in a powerful restatement of the opening theme in unison. Perhaps at the end of his career Koromzay was in as much need of reassurance as I was at the beginning of mine. We played an unhappy sort of chamber music, neither person providing the support the other craved.

I walked over to Koromzay and touched him lightly on the arm. 'Sorry I have to go now but I'll see you at Fay's house concert next week.'

'This music is hard – you will spend a lifetime working on it. It'll be better soon.' He looked up at me with the hint of a smile. 'I hope you can stay longer next time.'

In the small space between our music stands and the first row of audience, two black poodles sporadically crossed the room, collars rattling. Behind Fay Shwayder sat the new Dean of the College of Music, Daniel Sher, and his predecessor, Robert Fink, who had been responsible for structuring the original Takács residency funded by Fay at the University of Colorado. Further back I could hear Dénes Koromzay clearing his throat. At the end of the first piece he muttered to his neighbour, 'The boys are sounding good, but sometimes too fast.'

Concerts at Fay Shwayder's house took place in the large living room that housed her Asian art collection. Despite the generous quantity of Persian carpets on the floor that might otherwise have deadened the sound of string instruments, wooden cathedral ceilings ensured warm, lively acoustics. Fay's home was situated on a large plot of land adjoining the Green Gables Country Club in Lakewood, a suburb west of Denver. The west-facing windows looked out onto Ward Reservoir, the peak of Mount Evans visible in the distance. Fay and her partner, Harry Campbell, usually invited around forty of their friends and family for an hour of music followed by a buffet-style dinner.

In October 1993 we finished our concert at Fay's house with a quartet composed by Beethoven's primary teacher in Vienna, Haydn. During an extended residency in London in 1791–2, arranged by the entrepreneurial violinist, Johann Peter Salomon, Haydn attended public quartet concerts that were performed in the spacious Hanover Square Rooms by the Salomon Quartet. Upon his return to Vienna in 1793 Haydn composed his three Opus 74 quartets with a larger space in mind, sometimes adding richer sonorities and passages of increased virtuosity while other sections retained the intimacy of his earlier quartets.

In order to catch the attention of a larger and noisier audience in a public setting Haydn began each of these new quartets with a loud, emphatic statement. In Fay's house the two loud chords at the beginning of Opus 74, no. 1 were not needed for this purpose: Fay had already introduced us and the guests sat on foldable grey metal chairs waiting quietly for us to begin.

Throughout the first movement I was aware of the incongruity of playing this more extrovert music in such a small space. Were the joyful *forte* arrivals uncomfortably direct for our audience? Did the flurries of virtuosic passagework Haydn assigned to the first violin, doubtless with Salomon in mind, sound too edgy for the acoustic? As we continued to play we instinctively lightened our bowstrokes in the louder passages while in the quieter moments we enjoyed not having to project the character of the music, handing off a *grazioso* motif to each other in the *Andantino* second movement with less emphasis than usual – now the interchange seemed no more than an extension of the casual snippets of conversations we had heard between the assembled guests while we waited to begin the concert.

Towards the end of the high-spirited last movement of Opus 74, no. 1, a *crescendo* culminated in a dramatic unresolved chord and a suspenseful pause. What next? The clink of silverware from the kitchen and an aroma of stir-fry and dumplings invaded the silence. We continued with a hushed, chattering *pianissimo*, ignoring the previous drama. But before the mood could be comfortably established, an ebullient interruption shattered the quiet; the first violin melody was given an unmistakably rustic flavour by offbeat rhythms in the middle parts and a drone in the cello part which András highlighted by adding bow accents to his sustained note – a squeezebox effect. Three final emphatic chords brought the piece to a gutsy conclusion. Having delicately traversed the space between a private concert setting and a more public space, Haydn's quartet seemed to end outside, as if it was being played by a folk band inviting villagers to revel.

While the audience applauded, caterers had brought food out onto a long table adjacent to the audience – an effortless transition from music to dining. For Fay and her friends a string quartet concert was the reason for the gathering, but food and conversation were integral to the occasion. As a younger woman Fay had idolised artists such as the free-spirited dancer Isadora Duncan, whose bohemian lifestyle was the envy of a girl brought up in a more conservative and business-oriented environment. Primarily motivated by a desire to help enable a thriving local arts scene, Fay also enjoyed spending time with musicians and living vicariously our more itinerant way of life.

Once I had become accustomed to the proximity of poodles and patrons I began to look forward greatly to these concerts. We played at Fay's house several times during my first years in the quartet. The experience of trying out new repertoire in this supportive setting helped me to become gradually more confident in my new role.

At the end of Beethoven's first year in Vienna, Haydn wrote a letter to Beethoven's benefactor and employer in Bonn, the Elector of Cologne, Archduke Maximilian Franz. Haydn requested that the Elector increase Beethoven's allowance and enclosed a handful of compositions by his pupil: 'I flatter myself that these pieces, which are recommended as proof of the diligence that he applied beyond his actual studies, will most graciously be accepted by Your Serene Electoral Highness.'[8] The Elector replied none too serenely that, with the exception of one fugue, he recognised all of the enclosed music as having been composed and performed by Beethoven while still in Bonn: perhaps therefore it would be better for the devious student to terminate his seemingly redundant Viennese studies before he acquired more debt.

Even if Beethoven had been intending at some point to return to Bonn, the advances of the French army in 1794 made it impractical. A French victory over Austria at the battle of Fleurus in June marked a decisive turning point in the Revolutionary Wars. The Habsburg emperor, Franz II, decided to stop defending Austrian territory in the Netherlands and returned to his court in Vienna, allowing the French army to expand northwards. Following the French occupation of Bonn in the autumn, the Elector of Cologne dissolved his court, fled to Vienna and discontinued

Beethoven's allowance. With the dissolution of the court and the drying up of future professional possibilities for Beethoven in Bonn, the backing of new friends and patrons in Vienna became critical to his financial well-being and artistic development.

From 1794 Prince Lichnowsky facilitated new opportunities for Beethoven by holding chamber music concerts at his home every Friday morning. It was here that Beethoven got to know some of Vienna's leading string players, including the violinist Ignaz Schuppanzigh. Schuppanzigh was well placed to react to a changing environment for musicians, making opportunities for himself in much the same way that Salomon was doing in London. Benefitting from Lichnowsky's patronage, Schuppanzigh supplemented his income by teaching and increasing his involvement in public concerts. In 1795, when he was only eighteen years old, Schuppanzigh became director of a concert series in the Augarten which, initially designed for the private use of the emperor, had become a public garden in 1775. A famous restaurant owner, Ignaz Jahn, had opened a restaurant there in 1782 and encouraged its use for concerts, his continued backing reducing the financial risk for Schuppanzigh. Until the emergence of formal concert societies later in the nineteenth century, promoting public concerts would be the financial responsibility of players and composers, often backed by Viennese aristocrats keen to present their protégés to a wider audience. Over the course of the next twenty-five years Schuppanzigh would emerge as a prominent violinist, concert presenter and the musician most closely associated with Beethoven's quartets.

Lichnowsky paid Schuppanzigh and others to perform at his private chamber music concerts, support that helped solidify Beethoven's relationships with Vienna's best musicians as he started to compose music for small ensembles. Franz Wegeler, a childhood friend of Beethoven's from Bonn who lived in Vienna between 1794 and 1796, described the interactions at Lichnowsky's chamber music gatherings. During his earliest interactions with Viennese musicians Beethoven was apparently an amenable colleague, happy to accept the suggestions of the players. The famous cellist Anton Kraft pointed out to him that he should mark the passage in the finale of the third trio, Opus 1, with *sulla corda C* (the passage to be fingered only on the C string, producing a darker sonority), and that in the second of these trios the finale, which Beethoven had marked 4/4, should be changed to 2/4.[9]

Twenty-seven years older than Schuppanzigh, Kraft had been principal cellist in the now disbanded Esterházy orchestra and was the cellist for whom Haydn composed his second cello concerto, in D major. Kraft enhanced his reputation as a soloist by embarking on several concert tours at different stages of his career and became closely involved with Beethoven's first chamber works. Nonetheless this musician from an older generation than Beethoven and Schuppanzigh finished his career in Vienna in the service of the Bohemian noble, Prince Joseph Lobkowitz, who maintained one of the few remaining private orchestras.

The trios Kraft advised Beethoven on became his first published works, the three Opus 1 Piano Trios that he dedicated to Prince Lichnowsky. In this way Beethoven acknowledged his debt to the prince, who not only invited the composer to move from his first cramped lodgings into the Lichnowsky family's residence but also, by studying and playing his works, sought to encourage his protégé's unique compositional style.

The lively dialogue, humour and dramatic dynamic contrasts of Beethoven's first trios demonstrated that he had already learnt much from Haydn's earlier chamber music. When Haydn requested that Beethoven write 'Pupil of Haydn' at the top of his trios, however, the headstrong composer refused, saying, according to his friend Ferdinand Ries, that 'he had never learned anything from him'.[10]

Beethoven's resentment towards those to whom he owed most was not confined to Haydn. While he appreciated Lichnowsky's support he nonetheless sought to assert his independence. When he overheard the prince instructing his footman to serve Beethoven first if they should happen to ring at the same time, Beethoven immediately hired his own servant. When Beethoven decided to learn to ride, he chose to hire a horse of his own rather than borrow one from the Prince's stables.[11] Beethoven often preferred to eat independently at a tavern rather than be obliged to shave and dress more formally for dinner with his patron's family. He stayed with the Lichnowskys until at least 1795 but dissatisfaction with his living arrangements would later become a recurrent theme, causing him to change lodgings some thirty times during his thirty-five years in Vienna.

Although Beethoven at times grew frustrated with his benefactors, and with the niceties of social etiquette a musician dependent on the goodwill of aristocrats was obliged to follow, he showed no obvious signs of revolutionary fervour. Not until August 1794 did Beethoven mention the political situation in his letters: 'Here various important people have been locked up; it is said that a revolution was about to break out . . . People say that the gates leading to the suburbs are to be closed at 10 p.m. The soldiers have loaded their muskets with ball. You dare not raise your voice here or the police will take you into custody.'[12]

The crackdown by Emperor Franz II and his ministers that summer was inspired in part by an Austrian army lieutenant, Franz Hebenstreit, who admitted to an agent of the secret police a plot to overthrow the monarchy. Forty-five people were arrested and although their plan was vague, the Jacobin trials resulted in seven executions and many long prison sentences.[13] Even in the midst of such tumult Beethoven sensed a certain continuity in Viennese priorities: 'We are having very hot weather here; and the Viennese are afraid that soon they will not be able to get any more ice cream . . . I believe that so long as an Austrian can get his brown ale and his little sausages, he is not likely to revolt.'[14]

Beethoven's reticence about politics was probably prompted by a wish to avoid the attention of the secret police, and also encouraged by the benefits the prevailing social system offered him, however uncomfortably such privileges grated with his pride. Count Waldstein's letter of introduction had granted Beethoven entry to the highest echelons of Viennese society. With the support of patrons such as Prince Lichnowsky he was able to build on his reputation as a virtuosic pianist to become Vienna's most exciting young composer. In 1796 Beethoven felt sufficiently established in Vienna to write to his brother, 'I am well, very well. My art is winning me friends and renown, and what more do I want? And this time I shall make a good deal of money.'[15]

While Beethoven enjoyed his improved status in Vienna, continued French military victories fostered an atmosphere of increased distrust. The Austrian government curtailed intellectual freedoms, including closing reading rooms and circulation libraries. Emperor Franz was so concerned about the possibility of unrest that he forbade performances of music ensembles containing more than two people without prior police approval.[16] For Beethoven the spirit of change would be expressed through his musical evolution. By 1799 he felt ready to tackle the string quartet, eager to stamp his mark on a genre previously dominated by Haydn and Mozart and to utilise the musicians at his disposal in Lichnowsky's home. Violinist Louis Sina and violist Franz Weiss joined Schuppanzigh and Anton Kraft to become the first configuration of the Schuppanzigh Quartet. Emperor Franz may have sought to restrict gatherings of more than two people in public places but he need not have worried about Lichnowsky's Friday morning concerts where, as the eighteenth century drew to a close, the radical ideas being fomented were of a musical rather than a political nature.

I was back at Koromzay's house listening to the third movement of the Hungarian Quartet's recording of Opus 18, no. 1. Using a standard ABA form, Beethoven confounded expectations about the traditional role of the middle section. After a fleeting scherzo that featured lively interplay between all four parts, the Trio, more often functioning as a contrasting lyrical section, opened with a bludgeoning *fortissimo*, everyone playing the same notes and rhythms. The *fortissimo* propelled the first violinist into a mad dash, left-hand fingers obliged to move so quickly that mine often felt as if they would get tangled up with each other. Zoltán Székely, the first violinist of the

Hungarian Quartet, executed the passage effortlessly on the record.

'Thirty-five years is a long time to play with any first violinist. He was a great musician and a clever man – hard to argue with. Quiet but sometimes obstinate.' Koromzay lit a cigarette.

'Beethoven wrote an earlier version of this piece and later corrected this passage to make the first violin part more difficult.' Koromzay chuckled. 'It's a small change but in the second half Beethoven adds some big leaps and difficult string crossings with the bow. The effect is more extreme: the first violin has to live more dangerously. Maybe Beethoven wanted the violinist to show off a bit more, or perhaps he wanted to humble him – that's necessary sometimes. Zoltán was a great leader but there are different ways to be a first violinist. After we disbanded I formed another group from younger friends and colleagues, the New Hungarian Quartet. That was my quartet and the rehearsals were enjoyable. I will give you our recording of the Bartóks to listen to – it's a CD. I am sure you have a CD player. That's the recording I'm proudest of.'[*]

The idea that there might be more than one way of being a first violinist, which in turn would affect the artistic expression of the whole quartet, was liberating, one of many helpful insights that Koromzay shared with me about quartet playing until his death in 2001.[17] Rather than attempting the impossible task of emulating the multiple strengths of my predecessor I could view my arrival as a

---

[*] The New Hungarian Quartet played from 1972 to 1979. Koromzay was joined by Andor Toth, first violin, Richard Young, second violin and Andor Toth Junior as cellist.

chance for the group to rebalance roles and relationships.

I began to think more about how the music highlighted the different roles demanded of a first violinist. Clearly a section such as the flying runs at the beginning of this Trio, as with the virtuosic passagework Haydn had composed for Salomon several years earlier, required confident individualistic playing, while the unison opening of the whole piece demanded a more cooperative approach. I imagined the first players of this music facing a similar need to adapt to the music. Schuppanzigh would have been eager to impress both Beethoven and Prince Lichnowsky with his individual ability as a violinist, but quartets were a social endeavour: perhaps the young Schuppanzigh would have had to tread carefully with the more senior and experienced Anton Kraft. Forming good relationships with his colleagues would have been as essential to the success of the ensemble then as it was for me now.

Never allowing me to feel my junior status, Karcsi, Gábor and András were also generous with their time outside rehearsals. András and Karcsi frequently invited me to dinners resplendent with Hungarian specialities cooked by their wives Kati and Mari. Their children did not seem to mind the presence of a strange person around the dinner table, although Karcsi's youngest daughter alerted me to the fact that I had a very weird English accent. Not any more so than her dad's, I replied. Recently divorced, Gábor demonstrated a boyish excitement for the variety of fast-food options Boulder had to offer, with Taco Bell and Kentucky Fried Chicken heading his list. Once he took me to a shopping mall, eager to canvass my opinion on a grey suit he was considering buying for an upcoming lunchtime concert: this would be the only time anyone in the group consulted me for fashion advice.

I quickly understood András' statement that I would be joining a family. Wes Blomster, a professor of German and the local music critic, allowed me to stay in his apartment until I found a place of my own, providing me with a useful reading list including Joseph Kerman's incomparable book *Beethoven's Quartets*. Sabine Schaffner, who had grown up in my home town of Cambridge, and before her retirement worked at the Laboratory for Atmospheric and Space Physics at the University of Colorado, invited me to afternoon tea served on elegant bone china. A knowledgeable and encouraging listener, she tentatively suggested that in an early performance of a late Schubert quartet my sound might be too strident to bring out the lyrical qualities of the work. Agnes Persson, a Hungarian woman in her seventies who had grown up in Budapest in the 1920s with the sounds of the Waldbauer String Quartet rehearsing in her parents' living room, skipped the small talk when I first met her for lunch. 'Renting is for students. Here's a loan for $20,000 for a down payment: the boys need stability.' I declined the staggeringly generous offer while trying to reassure her that my intentions were honourable – by now I understood that joining a string quartet was no one-night stand.

Becoming one of the Takács boys, beloved by a local community who cared passionately about the quartet's future, was sometimes daunting. While I appreciated that so many people were willing to be welcoming, I felt like the recently acquired striker of a football team whose fans enthusiastically celebrate his arrival as they wait expectantly for him to score his first goals. Sometimes I turned down kind invitations, doubtless seeming less forthcoming and certainly less fun than the Hungarians as I struggled to balance the intensity of social and musical interactions.

The others were always willing to reassure me about the pressures of our way of life. 'We should just enjoy our work together,' András said in response to a bad review of one of our first concerts. 'It takes time but soon the audience will hear that in our playing.'

'I do feel like a reserved Englishman! I'm afraid it comes out in the music.'

'Sometime we're too much fun,' Karcsi said, grinning unapologetically. 'But if something goes wrong onstage, we have to laugh; don't take it too seriously.'

'You can't always feel good,' said Gábor. 'But we can help each other. And we'll be together for a long time. Don't worry.'

From his earliest days in Vienna Beethoven associated some of his compositions with friendship – a means by which to repair a disagreement or cement a relationship threatened by separation. One year after his arrival in Vienna, the twenty-three-year-old composer wrote to Eleonore von Breuning, his piano student and close child-hood friend in Bonn. Beethoven blamed himself for a quarrel between them and hoped he could make amends by dedicating a short piano piece to her. In a lighter vein Beethoven composed his duet for viola and cello, 'With Two Eyeglasses Obbligato', to play with his friend, the amateur Viennese cellist Nikolaus Zsemskall – both men were short-sighted.

In the second half of 1798, the Bohemian Prince Franz Joseph Maximilian von Lobkowitz – himself a competent singer, violinist and cellist – commissioned both the ageing

Haydn and his talented student to write six string quartets. Haydn would compose only the two Opus 77s and the unfinished Opus 103, hindered by other obligations and failing health. Towards the end of 1798 Beethoven began work on what would become his six Opus 18 quartets, and had probably finished them by 18 October 1800, when he received the second instalment of a fee totalling four hundred florins from Prince Lobkowitz.[18] This was a significant sum, more than half the amount it is estimated that someone in Beethoven's situation would have needed to support himself for a year.[19]

Beethoven's work on his new quartets became intertwined with old and new relationships. By 25 June 1799, he had finished the first version of Opus 18, no. 1 and gave it as 'a small token' of friendship to Karl Amenda, a violinist with whom he had become friends following Amenda's arrival in Vienna in spring 1798. Amenda was a year older than Beethoven and had trained in Lutheran theology at the University of Jena. After he moved to Vienna, he became the music teacher of Mozart's children. Later in the summer of 1799, the death of his brother forced Amenda to return to his home town of Courland, in Latvia. In honour of their friendship Beethoven made him a gift of Opus 18, no. 1, entreating him to remember the times they had spent together.[20]

Beethoven complained to Amenda at this time of a broken heart,[21] likely caused not so much by Amenda's imminent departure as by the marriage plans of one of Beethoven's piano students, Josephine von Brunsvik. In May that year, Josephine's mother Anna had brought Josephine and her sister Therese to Vienna and persuaded Beethoven to give them piano lessons. Beethoven's acquaintance with the family and possible infatuation with Josephine seems to have caused an interruption to his work on Opus 18, no. 1.[22] Five years later, after the death of Josephine's first husband, Beethoven would repeatedly declare his love for her, recalling that when he had first met her in 1799 he had been determined not to let himself fall in love. It seems rather more likely that Josephine was responsible for discouraging his overtures than that the young musician heroically repressed the desires of his heart. Whether or not her impending marriage was the cause of Beethoven's distress in the summer of 1799, Beethoven fell in love easily and frequently: a broken heart was a common emotional state for the sensitive composer who craved depth and intensity in his relationships.

Amenda's departure from Vienna may have contributed to Beethoven's anguish. Over a year later, Amenda wrote to Beethoven explaining that he had fallen in love and was likely to settle for good in Courland, but that when he played or listened to Beethoven's music, 'All of the ardent feelings awaken in me in the liveliest manner, [feelings] that your company itself inspired in me. It seems to me as if I must then get away from here and go to you, to the source of my most tender and most animated sentiments.'[23] Amenda feared – correctly – that they might never see each other again, and entreated Beethoven never to forget him.

The overt emotion in Amenda's letter was reciprocated. In the summer of 1801 Beethoven shared a painful secret with him:

How often would I like to have you here with me, for your B is leading a very unhappy life and is at variance with Nature and his Creator. Many times already I have cursed Him for exposing His creatures to the slightest hazard, so that the most beautiful blossom is thereby often crushed and destroyed. Let me tell you that my most prized possession, my hearing, has greatly deteriorated. When you were still with me, I already felt the symptoms; but I said nothing about them. Now they have become very much worse.[24]

Franz Wegeler was another of only a few close friends in whom Beethoven confided: 'For almost two years I have ceased to attend any social functions, just because I find it impossible to say to people: I am deaf.'[25]

Beethoven's professional situation, however, was now much better than it had been during his first years in Vienna. Publishers competed to publish his works, and as a result he was able to charge a higher fee for his compositions. He could now afford his own apartment and servant, although this increased independence was itself facilitated by Prince Lichnowsky, who paid him an annuity of six hundred gulden (or florins).

Some time after the composition and publication of Opus 18, Lichnowsky further demonstrated his belief in Beethoven's string quartet projects by purchasing a quartet of Italian string instruments for him: violins by Joseph Guarnerius and Nicolò Amati, a viola by Vincenzo Rugeri and a cello by Andreas Guarnerius.[26] The seal of Beethoven, stamped under the neck of the instruments, must not have seemed adequate proof of ownership: Beethoven took matters into his own hands, scratching a big B on the back of each instrument.[27] Although Beethoven himself played the violin and viola, given his hearing problems it seems most likely that the primary beneficiaries of this purchase would have been Schuppanzigh and his quartet colleagues.

Thus Beethoven composed his Opus 18 quartets at a time when considerable professional recognition could not keep at bay feelings of social isolation, caused in large part by his increased deafness and frustrations about his Viennese friends, many of whom he dared not tell about his condition. To Amenda he worried not so much about the danger to his professional abilities as about the devastating effect on his social interactions.[28] In 1824 Goethe would describe a string quartet as 'four rational people conversing with each other'.[29] Grieving the loss of companionship, Beethoven created his own ideal dialogues in his Opus 18 quartets, conversations over which he had complete control.

Koromzay had alerted me to the two different versions of Opus 18, no. 1, differentiated in no uncertain terms by Beethoven in the same letter to Amenda in which he had lamented the deterioration in his hearing: he entreated his friend not to share the earlier version with anybody; when he received the newest version he would surely notice that only now had Beethoven learned the art of quartet writing.[30]

Eagerly I compared the two, searching for evidence to back up Beethoven's seemingly exaggerated statement. One obvious difference was in the tempo markings: in the last movement Beethoven chose a more extreme marking to increase vivacity; *Allegretto* became *Allegro*. The change to the slow movement had more to do with character: *Adagio molto* became *Adagio affettuoso ed appassionato* – 'very slow' becoming 'slow, tenderly and passionately'. In both cases Beethoven's intention seemed to be to make the music more vivid, but the responsibility for implementing these changes lay in the hands of the performers.

Beethoven made some of the more significant composi-tional alterations in the development section of the first movement. This is the section roughly one third of the way through a sonata-form movement where a composer has the greatest licence to digress into remote keys and textures, dissecting and transforming themes. In one section of dia-logue in Beethoven's original version, the order of entries proceeded predictably from the bottom to the top of the group: cello, viola, second violin and finally first violin, each entering one bar after the previous instrument. In the final version Beethoven amended the order, the first violin jumping his turn, coming in after the viola. As if outraged by his presumption, the second violin entered a mere one beat later. The changes made the dialogue seem more spon-taneous, both violins in their own way breaking the rules of engagement established by the cello and viola. When we rehearsed this section we exaggerated the interruptions: each player came in slightly ahead of the beat, the musical equivalent of an argument where people become increas-ingly heated and refuse to wait their turn.

These and other changes to phrase lengths and textures served to clarify the musical line and lend the music more dramatic impact, but I couldn't find the differences as dras-tic as Beethoven had implied. In its original form the piece was absolutely recognisable. If Beethoven had made no further changes to the original manuscript he gave to Amenda, it would nonetheless have stood well alongside the other Opus 18 quartets. The changes were not as extreme as Beethoven described them to his friend, but in his mind the spirit of transformation was already central to his compositional process – a fact that would become shock-ingly apparent in his later quartets.

Beethoven's revised instruction to play the *Adagio* tenderly and passionately made me re-examine the violin melody at the beginning of the slow movement. Karl Amenda described this movement as portraying the 'parting of two lovers', a comment gratifying to Beethoven, who claimed to have been inspired by the tomb scene in *Romeo and Juliet* and had written an inscription in French, *Les derniers soupirs* (the last breaths), in an early draft.[31]

While the others played a repeated rhythm I was assigned a beautiful melody above. What were the particular features of the tune that could be brought out to increase passion or tenderness? An unusually long note at the beginning built suspense; the longer it continued the more the note seemed to ask what would come next. A singer would change her sound toward the end of the long first note so that the next would seem to come inevitably out of the first. On the violin I could achieve this by increasing the speed of my vibrato as the note developed.

In the most expressive gesture, towards the end of the phrase, a short scale led up to the highest note of the phrase, a B flat, followed by a plunge down a diminished seventh, a far larger interval than anything before:

A good singer would underscore the distance between the two by filling it in with some sort of slide between the notes. This technique could be imitated on the violin only by climbing high up the fingerboard on the A string and allowing the finger playing the top note to linger on the string during the shift downwards to the lower note, as if reluctant to leave its post.

When we first rehearsed the piece together in Boulder I was excited to try out my melody. We got as far as the first four bars before András stopped playing.

'Let's play this without Ed.'

'Maybe we're too slow,' said Gábor. *Még egyszer*. 'Once again' was a more useful expression in the Takács studio than *nagyon szép* (very nice), which had met with general hilarity when I first tried it out on my colleagues.

'Don't we sound too short and restless?' said András. He played a smoother version of the accompaniment. 'What's the English word: unsub-tle?' Their English was improving a great deal faster than my Hungarian.

'Sounds sleepy,' Karcsi said. 'More *appassionato*!'

'But *husika*, it should be sad, just the start of the story, not a hurricane,' said András. *Husika* – 'sweetie pie' – reminded me of my teacher Dorothy DeLay's use of 'sugar plum' to preface a particularly trenchant criticism.

'Sorry, Ed, this accompaniment is hard,' said Gábor. 'What do you think?'

I suggested that they all use a slightly faster bow speed nearer the fingerboard to create a breathless yet hushed sound. '*Nagyon szép*,' said Karcsi, with the hint of a smirk.

Even when a melody in the first violin part was accompanied by the other three parts, the communication of mood was a group endeavour. While I held my opening long note, the others would determine the pulse and momentum. By the time I played my next note the character would already be established by the accompaniment. In a passage that I had identified as being dominated by the first violin, the mood of the music was equally the responsibility of the other parts. Developing a strong concept for how to play my melody was a good beginning; now I could allow it to be further affected by the mood of the accompaniment, individual and group expression complementing one another.

While I began to be more comfortable with the musical demands of my new position, other aspects of the life of a touring musician were disorienting. Unusually for an ensemble based in the US, two-thirds of our concerts during my first season with the Takács were abroad. Between September 1993 and August 1994 we played sixty concerts: just over twenty in Europe during three separate visits, twenty in North America (including six in Boulder), and another twenty during a month-long tour of Australia and New Zealand. This represented a considerable decrease in engagements for a group that had been accustomed to playing as many as a hundred concerts a year. As a result we agreed to several concerts at the last minute that winter, even when the distance between venues was not ideal. Santiago de Compostela was thus scheduled after a concert in Indianapolis. We flew to Spain overnight, travelled by car up to Santiago, slept for an hour and played the concert, the first of eight on consecutive nights – three in Spain followed by five in Ireland. The next day was a travel day before our first concert in London since I had joined the quartet.

The clock display read 5:00. It was already dark outside and I could hear the occasional car passing on the London street below my hotel room. I had slept through my alarm and had only thirty minutes to change into my concert clothes and walk to the Wigmore Hall for our stage rehearsal. With its fussy accessories a tuxedo was a cumbersome uniform: cufflinks resisting buttonholes and a bow tie that wouldn't stay straight. In due course I planned to raise the possibility of wearing a more comfortable outfit, but for now a pallid show of independence was born of necessity: with only one long black sock remaining in my suitcase a short brown one would have to make up the pair. From an adjoining room came an occasional snore. For a Saturday afternoon in central London there seemed to be extraordinarily little traffic. None of the usual interior sounds of a hotel – doors slamming, showers running, elevators opening – disturbed the calm. Nothing at all. I looked again at the clock display: 5:00 the red display showed, but the p.m. dot was not illuminated.

At 5:00 a.m. I was standing elegantly dressed in my tuxedo in the middle of my room. No stage rehearsal to rush to after all. Back in bed I tried to banish the awakenings of pre-concert adrenalin. The experience summed up the difficulties I had adjusting to quartet life on the road during my first year.

My expectations of travel had been formed to a large extent by childhood summer holidays. The night before departure my brother and I would be sent to bed early to be well rested for the journey. My parents had already chosen a route and packed so that we could leave in good time the next morning. We would avoid any ugly and dangerous motorways, taking in the most scenic parts of the English countryside in leisurely fashion. As lunchtime approached my mother assumed the responsibility of finding the perfect picnic place, up a small road away from traffic noise in a field with a view and no inquisitive cattle to distract from the consumption of cheese-and-tomato or ham-and-lettuce sandwiches, pork pies, fruit cake, chocolate bars, lemonade and coffee. These feasts were required only to satisfy our hunger until teatime, when a tea shop would be located in a picturesque village, serving English cream teas of jam scones with clotted cream or coffee cake. At the end of the journey we would be greeted by grandparents waiting outside the door of their country cottage, my brother and I finessing affectionate yet hasty reunions before rushing upstairs to see what welcome gifts had been laid out on our beds.

Such family journeys were like smooth musical transitions between two melodies or key centres: the distance from A to B negotiated with a few welcome and expected chord changes, agreeable rhythmic variety and a change of texture – a pleasant interlude with no doubt concerning the positive outcome.

When I first joined the Takács, the group owned a dirty white Ford Granada that András' brother maintained and delivered to Munich Airport for the beginning of a European tour. From there we would drive all over Europe, saving money on the five air tickets we would otherwise have had to purchase – the cello could not be checked in and required its own seat. With all the heavy luggage crammed into the trunk and the cello placed across the lucky laps of two people sitting in the back seats, the body of the car lifted up towards the front, as if it might at any moment take off. It was hard to experience the eleven-hour journey between Rotterdam and Budapest, undertaken after the previous night's concert and lengthy post-concert dinner, as a soothing transition. During my first year the amount of time spent travelling and the frequent, unpredictable delays caused by traffic jams, bad weather and plane cancellations contributed to my sense of disorientation.

As we drove across Europe the Hungarians described with zest previous setbacks on the road. When the old quartet car (reassuringly also a Ford Granada) had burst into flames on the French motorway, the alacrity with which the quartet extricated themselves and instruments was a source of pride, the sort of experience that added spice to touring life. Driving a hundred miles in the wrong direction late at night in Vermont, only to be alerted to their mistake by the surprising presence of Canadian customs officials, was a digression that merely added to the adventure.

Listening to these stories made it clear how much greater than mine was the Hungarians' taste for risk, how much more their relish for unpredictable transitions. Their greater spontaneity onstage reflected a more carefree and adventurous attitude to life; a willingness to embrace the uncertainties of journeys and not be so fixated on their outcome. They had experienced and adapted to far greater changes than I had: moving with their families from Budapest to Colorado and more recently accommodating an Englishman into the group with the accompanying necessity of rehearsing in a second language. Feeling nostalgic for home-made sandwiches consumed on a soft tartan rug overlooking an idyllic Cotswolds village wasn't likely to ease my integration into the group. In the short term I could do no more than be aware of my inadequacy, trying more fully to accept the unpredictability of life on the road, hoping that with time the flexible attitude of my colleagues would seep into my music-making onstage.

Towards the end of my first year in the quartet we travelled to Australia and New Zealand to play a tour of twenty concerts under the auspices of Musica Viva, Australia's national chamber music organisation, and Chamber Music New Zealand. Both organisations arranged our travel and hotels – an old Ford Granada was most sadly not at our disposal.

In Hobart, Tasmania, we visited the local radio station where the announcer promised two free tickets to the first listener who called in to name the maker of our instruments. Just as Lichnowsky had purchased a set of quartet instruments for Beethoven, we too had been the beneficiaries of such generosity. Since 1988 the Takács had been borrowing a 'matched' set of old Italian instruments by the Italian maker Amati, owned previously by Mrs William Andrews Clark and bequeathed to the Corcoran Gallery of Art in Washington DC in 1963. The term 'matched' was misleading, in the sense that they had not been matched by their maker nor indeed by the musicians who played them, but by Mrs Clark when she purchased them. In fact, although three of the instruments were made by Nicolò Amati, the violin I was playing on was made by his father, Hieronymo. The instruments shared a warm and silky character of sound, which was an asset both real and theoretical during my first year, when integration and blend were issues under scrutiny. When the Amati cello needed its yearly maintenance, András performed on an instrument by the modern maker Christopher Dungey. A review of one concert where András played the Dungey cello complimented the quartet on the remarkable blend of instruments, noting that such unanimity was clearly facilitated by the matched set of Amatis. The reputation of the Amati set influenced what people thought they heard.

At the end of the Australian tour we played the last

movement of Opus 18, no. 1 as an encore to conclude our concert in Launceston, Tasmania. With its brilliant cascading runs, lively interplay between the parts and rhythmic momentum, this finale made for an effective end to a concert. In the original version Beethoven gave to his friend Amenda, the violins generated the initial drive towards the final chords. But in the final version Beethoven redistributed the responsibility for excitement: now it was the second violin and viola who created the rhythmic drive with the first violin and cello commenting at half the speed.

In the final bars of both versions the second violin and viola threw back and forth the fast descending runs that had dominated the movement, but four bars before the end in the later version, the second violin and viola combined forces, creating a final collaborative flourish with their passagework. By intensifying the virtuosic brilliance in the middle voices right at the end of this dramatic piece, Beethoven gave notice of how important the relative roles of the instruments would become to his quartet project.

With his Opus 18 quartets, Beethoven intensified the interest and drama of the conversation between four individuals in a quartet. In my first year in the Takács Quartet, part of my evolution as a first violinist came from recognising how interconnected the four voices were: working with such lively and flexible colleagues allowed me to escape, at least at times, from the pressure of individual expectation and revel in the satisfactions of being part of something larger than myself. Playing twenty concerts during a four-week period also provided a boost to confidence; with less time to dwell on the challenges of the situation I began to relish the adventure of being a touring musician.

After the Launceston concert a woman approached me

backstage: 'Thank you for introducing the encore; it was wonderful to hear the Hungarian accent again.' Despite the wishful thinking of an audience member giving me a compliment entirely unrelated to my playing, this was by far the most gratifying feedback I had received all season. I was briefly one of a matched set of Hungarians, an illusion gratifyingly reinforced several months later by a review that complimented our playing of a Bartók quartet in a manner 'only possible by true-born Hungarians'. In both cases, perhaps, these reactions were made possible by the greater ease I was beginning to feel in the group, caused both by my musical experiences living the varied roles of a first violinist and by my supportive colleagues, setting me an example by their zestful, uninhibited attitudes to the changing life of a string quartet.

'It's been a good first season, sugar plum,' András said, with a characteristic raise of his eyebrows. 'How do you like your "job" so far?'

3

Fracture: Opus 59, no. 2

Gábor was laughing so hard that he could scarcely stand up to bow. The mishap occurred in February 1994 at the last concert of a music festival in Cuernavaca, Mexico, during one of my first performances of Opus 59, no. 2. In the *Più presto*, a breakneck conclusion to an already lively final movement, the first violin played the same galloping rhythm as the other instruments but one bar later. At the moment when we were supposed to begin playing the rhythm together I played a two-note figure one time too many. Unsure whether to accommodate my wayward-ness or ignore it in the hopes that I would catch up, my flexible colleagues effected a lethal combination of the two, some forging ahead, others holding back, then pursuing the alternative option as atonal mayhem ensued. We lurched along, now intent merely on managing one final chord together. After anxious glances around the group András seized the initiative, an emphatic lifting of his bow followed by a ferocious downward nod signalling that whatever anyone else was planning to play, this would be his last note. Our final sounds were almost executed together – a mishmash of scrambled pitches faintly resembling the emphatic E minor chord written by Beethoven.

It is a wise plan to finish any piece with a chord in the key intended by the composer. This is particularly true of the finale of Opus 59, no. 2 – the second of three quartets commissioned in 1805 by the Russian ambassador in

Vienna, Count Andrei Kirillovich Razumovsky – where at the beginning of the movement a raucously triumphant theme in the first violin, accompanied by a rhythm of galloping horses in the three other parts, invades in the 'wrong' key of C major. Since the first and third movements are in E minor and the second movement in E major, the conventional rules of composition would require the last movement also to be in E minor. But the C major impostor refuses to retreat; a ferocious tussle unfolds as E minor tries to reassert itself in the face of persistent regressions to C major.

Following a final *fortissimo* statement of the C major theme, the *Più presto* where I had lost my place returns the music to its rightful key, the C major invader finally repelled. The piece ends emphatically in E minor – in most performances.

Why had I lost my place? It wasn't just that the Opus 59s were more technically difficult than Beethoven's previous quartets. The exhilarating range and contrasts of emotion made it difficult to achieve the 'cool head and hot heart' that one of my violin teachers had prescribed as the ideal psychological state during performance. My pulse was already rushing from the ferocious C major outburst; with the additional excitement of the faster *Più presto* tempo a momentary doubt crept in. Would I still be able to control my fingers well enough? The loss of concentration was enough to cause the mistake.

In this finale excitement and danger went hand in hand. During two earlier whirlwind transitions that prepared the way for returns of the C major theme we threw a three-note figure frantically around the quartet, each counting like mad so as to enter at the right moment:

Every entrance was critical; missing your turn would put off the next participant, the music suddenly faltering like a time-delayed conversation on a transatlantic phone line, each person waiting for the other to begin, then both talking at once. Awareness of the potential dangers of the passage could easily become a self-fulfilling prophecy: I had to force myself to play with more courage, relishing the invigorating interchanges, enjoying the risks involved. The music challenged me to overcome fearfulness, to play with greater vitality yet more control. I was not yet well enough prepared to meet the demands of Opus 59, no. 2. This was music that required both a cooler head and a hotter heart.

The first audiences and players to encounter Beethoven's middle-period compositions, including the Opus 59 quartets, were not always appreciative of the challenges the music presented. Commenting on the first semi-public performance of Beethoven's Third Symphony ('Eroica'), which had taken place on 20 January 1805 (following private performances in Prince Lobkowitz's palace), a critic from a Leipzig-based newspaper, the *Allgemeine musikalische Zeitung*, drew a stark comparison. In Beethoven's

First Symphony, 'an uncommon richness of beautiful ideas are charmingly and splendidly developed, and overall pervades continuity, order and light'. The Third Symphony, by contrast, 'is written in a completely different style . . . [and] often it loses itself in lawlessness'. There is 'too much that is glaring and bizarre, which hinders greatly one's grasp of the whole, and the sense of unity is almost completely lost'.[1]

Viennese audiences in 1805 had good reason to crave order and light from their music. Between 16 and 19 October Napoleon defeated the Austrian army at the battle of Ulm and began to advance towards Vienna. Henry Reeve, an Englishman visiting Vienna at the time, noted that theatre directors wished to close their theatres during this alarming time, 'but the magistrate ordered them to be open, and the people are to be amused whether they will or no'.[2] On 13 November, thousands of French cavalry and infantry soldiers marched through Vienna. Four days later a thousand Austrian prisoners were marched into town. 'Nothing certain is known . . . all posts stopped; every channel of information shut up; we are surrounded by armies on every side.'[3]

During November Reeve attended one of the first performances of Beethoven's new opera, *Fidelio*. Intimidated by the French occupation, the Viennese public stayed away. A paltry audience was made up of French officers and a few of Beethoven's friends. According to Reeve *Fidelio* did not provide the enforced amusement imagined by the Viennese magistrate: 'Intricacy is the character of Beethoven's music, and it requires a well practised ear or the frequent repetition of the same piece, to understand and distinguish its beauties.'[4]

The Russian ambassador in Vienna, Count Razumovsky, could consider himself as the proud owner of two well-practised ears. A keen amateur violinist, he had been immersed in Viennese cultural life before becoming ambassador in 1792. In 1788 he had married Elizabeth, Countess Thun, whose mother, Maria Wilhelmine, was a prominent member of the Austrian aristocracy and presided over a musical salon frequented by Haydn and Mozart. Countess Thun's sister Maria Christiane was married that same year to Prince Lichnowsky. After Razumovsky arrived in Vienna to assume his diplomatic position in 1792 he enjoyed playing Haydn's string quartets and most likely attended the chamber music concerts hosted by his brother-in-law at which the Opus 18 quartets were first rehearsed and performed.

Towards the end of 1805 Count Razumovsky commissioned Beethoven to compose three new string quartets. The first two would each include a Russian folk song, chosen by Beethoven either out of respect to his patron or because Razumovsky had requested them. The concept of Russian patriotism must have seemed particularly poignant at the time: in December Tsar Alexander's decision to follow the advice of the Austrian General Weyrother instead of his own General Kutuzov, described so vividly in *War and Peace*, led to the overwhelming defeat of the Austrian and Russian armies by Napoleon at the battle of Austerlitz. Henry Reeve described the aftermath: 'Russian prisoners are marched into Vienna, poor miserable ragged wretched objects: the hospitals, convents, and schools are filled with the wounded from both [French and Russian] armies.'[5]

Beethoven selected two folk songs from his edition of a recently published collection of Russian tunes by Ivan

Prach. The concluding text for the first melody, presented by the cello at the beginning of the last movement of Opus 59, no. 1, was hardly rousing recruiting material:

> Madam, good mother!
> It wasn't my wife who caused me to age,
> It wasn't my little children,
> But what aged me, mother,
> Were the foreign, far-off lands,
> The Tsar's cruel [military] service,
> And all those frequent, distant military campaigns.[6]

It is not known if Beethoven understood the Russian text, but even if his choice was conscious he transformed the melancholy character of the slow folk tune into a fast, lively romp. Beethoven only invoked the wistful nature of the original song just before the end of the piece, presenting the folk song in a slow tempo before displacing it with a jubilant flourish – a final defiant gesture doubtless appreciated by Razumovsky during this grim period.[7]

Like most of Beethoven's patrons, Count Razumovsky responded to the turbulent times by maintaining an extravagant lifestyle, ignoring the threats to the aristocratic way of life posed by the French Revolution and the rise of Napoleon. Razumovsky marked himself apart from other members of the Viennese nobility, most of whom lived in the central area of Vienna, by purchasing a large parcel of land outside the city walls on a hill overlooking the Donau canal. He began to build a palace in the classical style of such grandeur as to be a suitable venue to host Tsar Alexander I during his visits to Vienna. Instead of choosing a more conventional French Baroque style of garden with its formal geometric design, Razumovsky employed the most famous gardener of the day, Konrad Rosenthal, to create an English garden, freer and more romantic in its conception. The palace would look over grassland areas, trees, streams and an open-air theatre while a new bridge over the canal would provide easy access to the Prater, Vienna's largest park and recreational area. By the time Razumovsky commissioned Beethoven to compose three new quartets the palace was nearly complete, its façade of columns and pilasters dominating the surrounding area.

Razumovsky planned to fill his new palace with fine art and music. One room would house his growing collection of sculptures by the Italian sculptor Canova, while a garden wing would feature a library for his rare manuscript collection and a concert hall, known as the White Hall. By commissioning Beethoven to compose the quartets the count continued his project to position himself as an avid supporter of the arts.

The rise of the Razumovsky family had itself been facilitated by an act of musical patronage. While travelling through rural Ukraine in 1731 a nobleman from St Petersburg was impressed by the fine bass voice of a twenty-one-year-old Ukrainian peasant singing in a local choir. The nobleman recruited Alexei Razumovsky – Count Andrei's uncle – for a church choir in St Petersburg. Elizabeth, Empress of Russia, was the same age as Alexei and admired more than his voice. She appointed him to her own choir, became his lover and married him in a private ceremony, the last act inspiring his subsequent nickname 'the Emperor of the Night'. Elizabeth made Alexei a prince and field marshal, while out of respect to the Russian Empress, the

Emperor of Austria appointed him Count of the Holy Roman Empire in 1742.[8] Alexei's multiple talents had propelled him into the intimate circles of the Russian court. Benefitting from Alexei's position, his brother Kirill – Andrei's father – was promoted within the army.

Andrei emulated his father and uncle by developing close relations with royalty. Catherine the Great had succeeded her husband Peter III (Elizabeth's heir and nephew) in 1762. Andrei became best friends with Catherine's son Paul, and in 1773, when Andrei was twenty-one, began secretly plotting with Paul's wife Natalya to depose Catherine so that Paul could become Tsar. This touching if ineffectual show of loyalty was somewhat marred by Andrei simultaneously commencing an affair with Natalya.

The subsequent exposure of this affair may have provided the necessary impetus for the beginning of Razumovsky's career as a foreign diplomat, posted far from the machinations of the Russian court. After appointments in Copenhagen and Sweden, in 1792 the forty-year-old count arrived in Vienna to assume his position as Russian ambassador. Razumovsky's subsequent career would be at the mercy of the quixotic and temperamental personalities of the Tsars. He was dismissed in 1799 by Paul, who had become Tsar three years earlier, but following Paul's assassination in 1801 Razumovsky was reinstated by his brother, Tsar Alexander I. Throughout the subsequent ups and downs of his relationship with Alexander, Razumovsky's palace would sustain his position in Viennese society.

Beethoven began work on the quartets for Razumovsky in spring 1806. Late in the summer he visited Prince Lichnowsky at his castle on the Lichnowsky estate at Grätz

(modern Graz), roughly one hundred and forty miles
north-east of Vienna. The visit ended abruptly in October.
Lichnowsky had hosted a banquet for French officers based
in the area, at the end of which Beethoven was asked to
improvise on the piano. Beethoven resented being asked to
entertain on demand, particularly for the French audience.
Despite the repeated requests of his patron he refused to
oblige the guests, improvising instead a swift departure for
Vienna the very same evening. During the three-day journey a rainstorm left water stains on music in his trunk,
including the manuscript of the first two movements of
Opus 59, no. 2 and sketches for the following movements.[9]
Once back in his lodgings Beethoven apparently smashed a
bust of his most loyal patron onto his apartment floor.[10] The
dispute was probably responsible for the termination in the
same year of the 600-florin annuity that Lichnowsky had
been paying to Beethoven, although relations between the
two were at least partially repaired in subsequent years.[11]

In contrast with Lichnowsky, Beethoven's dealings with
Razumovsky seem to have been refreshingly straightforward. Razumovsky's requests were mild; if he did indeed
ask Beethoven to include Russian folk songs in his quartets,
this was a less offensive proposition than being asked to
play the piano for Napoleon's generals. Perhaps Razumovsky's skills as a diplomat helped him avoid the problems his brother-in-law had encountered: he maintained a
less personal association with Beethoven – and to be on the
safe side did not present a bust of himself to the composer.
In the years following the argument at Grätz, Razumovsky
would take the place of Lichnowsky as the most significant
champion of Beethoven's string quartets.

*

Beethoven had scratched his initials on the set of instruments given to him by Prince Lichnowsky but it was too late for us to do the same on the backs of the Amatis – in spring 1994 the director of the Corcoran Gallery of Art informed us that with looming financial challenges the gallery could no longer justify the costs of insuring and maintaining musical instruments. The instruments had to be purchased from the Corcoran or returned by the end of September. This was a significant setback: we had come to rely on the Corcoran's patronage and always looked forward to the three concerts a year we played in return at the gallery's Armand Hammer Auditorium, one of the most intimate and inspiring chamber music halls in North America. The Amatis seemed too expensive a proposition but in any case we would now have to either find a patron keen to invest in string instruments or become an a cappella vocal group.

We began our search by contacting instrument dealers in North America and England. All that we required were powerful-sounding instruments with a versatile tonal palette that could blend with each other as well as be distinctive individually, were comfortable to play and in great condition, the paperwork and provenance of which contained no ambiguities off-putting to an investor, that were better value for money than the Amatis, and that would be available as soon as possible – if we could find a patron to buy them. Oddly we didn't receive many return calls, but just enough dealers in Toronto, Chicago and London responded to give us some hope.

As we began to discuss the ideal attributes of quartet instruments we could now acknowledge some disadvantages of the Amatis. One violin was noticeably more powerful than the other, the viola had uncomfortably large dimensions and the cello sometimes lacked clarity in the lower registers. These silky-toned instruments sounded good in smaller halls but didn't have quite a big enough dynamic range for the larger venues. We found it relatively easy to create a smooth, blended quartet sound, but sometimes in passages where the clarity of individual lines was more important our sound was too homogeneous.

As a student I had found violin dealers intimidating, with their overly reverberant showrooms furnished with expensive Turkish carpets, heavy mahogany cases and publicity shots signed with glowing tributes by famous string players glittering on the walls. My insecurity was compounded by knowing very little about violins and violin-makers. I might as well have been in the market for a summer quilt or a pair of shoes when confronted with terms like 'original button', 'grand pattern' and 'flat arching'. Experts had a particular way of holding a violin while evaluating it, avoiding touching the body of the instrument by using one hand to hold the neck while the other lightly supported the violin at its base. This made it easy to rotate the instrument slowly from front to back, looking for clues as to its condition – no violin played for the last two hundred or more years would have survived without some major repair work. While assuming this discerning pose I examined a violin shown to me by the Chicago-based dealer Jim Warren, who had been introduced to us by Michael Remenyi, his business partner and a Hungarian friend of the quartet.

'That's a huge crack down the back. How does it affect the value?'

'It's not a repair but an example of a two-piece back:

those are more common than the one-piece back, but it doesn't affect the price. You can see it still has its original button.'

I resolved to ask no more questions. Jim spent the whole afternoon with us, and while acknowledging that he didn't yet have anything quite suitable, offered to collect instruments with Michael Remenyi and bring them to Boulder a couple of months later.

In September 1994 we assembled on the stage of Grusin Music Hall to try out violins. With the low-key cheerfulness of one proposing to buy us coffee, Fay Shwayder had intimated that if we selected suitable instruments, her family foundation would consider buying them for our use. We couldn't believe our luck. In the eight years since the Takács had moved to Boulder, Fay had been a generous but inconspicuous supporter, enjoying regular tennis matches with members of the quartet but never seeking to establish a close relationship or meddle in the day-to-day life of the group. Fay explained that her first priority would be buying a violin for Karcsi and a cello for András. Gábor's situation was less urgent: Clare Seidel, a subscriber to our Boulder concert series, had loaned him a fine viola by the Italian maker Carlo Landolfi. Fay wanted to get to know me a little better before considering a further instrument purchase.

Fay and her partner Harry Campbell sat next to Jim Warren and Michael Remenyi, who had brought four candidates for us to try. András had already selected from the London dealer, Charles Beare, a cello he loved that was made in 1760 by Giorgio Seraphin.

Karcsi and I played each instrument while András and

Gábor took up positions at the back of the hall. Their feedback would be essential – an instrument that sounds wonderful under the ear may not necessarily project into a larger space. After initial tests, two of the four violins stood out both as being more powerful and as having a warmer quality of sound. They were from the same maker, G. B. Guadagnini: one was made in 1755 during his time in Milan and the other in 1763 during his Parma period.

Comparing the two violins highlighted how personal the match is between a player and an instrument. When I tried the instruments the Milan violin sounded better, but when Karcsi played them the Parma violin was superior. With the second-violin quartet parts in mind and to complement his own tonal preferences, Karcsi was searching for a dark sound and resonant lower strings. Sensing these characteristics in the Parma Guadagnini, he was able to bring out the strengths of the instrument. I was looking for a brighter, more soprano sound that would sing more easily in the upper registers than the Amati I had been playing. Less interested by the darkness and depth of sound in the Parma instrument, I brought out the clear, sweet and lively character of the Milan Guadagnini.

András and Gábor joined us onstage to see how the violins would fare with the viola and cello. After playing extracts from quartets by Haydn and Bartók, we moved on to Opus 59, no. 2, to which we had returned in preparation for a concert later in autumn 1994 at the University of Chicago.

At the beginning of Beethoven's *Allegretto* third movement, the *pianissimo* melody in the first violin part provided a good test. Compared with the Amati I had played previously, the Guadagnini produced a more transparent, shiny sound that floated effortlessly above a rhythmic accompaniment. Because my muscles were accustomed to playing the previous instrument I had to remind myself not to dig out the sound; this violin responded better to coaxing than coercion.

Our first impression was that we could hear each other more clearly. Gábor and Karcsi's syncopated rhythm bounced more crisply off András' downbeats. The sudden dynamic changes from *piano* to *fortissimo* were easier to execute. The instruments gave an exciting sense of possibilities waiting to be explored.

Now we moved on to the *Maggiore* section where Beethoven had set the second of the two Russian folk songs for Razumovsky. Hearing the same melody played by each of the instruments would tell us how they worked next to each other. Gábor announced the sprightly *Thème russe*, the key now changing to the brighter-sounding E major – a courageous soldier singing as he marched, the text of the original song suitably patriotic:

> Glory to you, God in the heavens, Glory!
> To our Tsar on this earth, Glory!

Beethoven marked the theme *piano* for three bars, followed by a *crescendo* to a spiky *sforzando* at the end of the phrase and a retreat back to *piano*:

One after another, more soldiers joined in: Karcsi, András, and then I played the tune. Again Gábor took it over, followed by Karcsi and then András, his theme now doubled in the viola part and growing to *forte*, where Karcsi and I took it over. András entered one more time, *fortissimo*. Regimental procedure was joyfully abandoned: the viola interrupted the cello after András had played only a third of the cello theme. The second violin broke into the viola tune, the first violin barged into the second violin's line and then the cello contributed belligerent off-beat *sforzandi*. What had begun as orderly renditions of the folk song became a riotous free-for-all. Suddenly, as if a severe general had arrived to review the regiment, the rowdy soldiers produced a startlingly deferential *piano* version of the *Thème russe*, presented one last time but now smoothly, legato bow-strokes for the first time replacing the spiky short strokes that had been the dominant feature of the theme.

Gábor's Landolfi had a brighter sound than the Amati, suitable for this perky theme, but I wondered how a viola sound that turned more towards the violins than the cello would affect the overall tone quality of the ensemble. The viola plays a critical sonic role in the group, bridging the gap between the violins and cellos. An instrument that could work with the violins but also blend with the darker sounds of the cello when required would be ideal.

Karcsi's statement of the folk-song theme sounded more full-bodied than Gábor's, despite being in a somewhat higher register. The much lower cello entrance was dark and vibrant while my first violin statement sounded clear and powerful. Playing on a more robust-sounding violin I didn't have to work so hard: the Guadagnini felt like an ally already, responding to a less muscular bowing arm technique with a resounding tone. In the subsequent joyful interruptions where we all piled in on top of each other, Gábor's viola seemed at a slight disadvantage. The other three instruments, however, seemed to give us a greater independence and more possibility of exulting in the argument between the voices.

Razumovsky should have been delighted by the prolonged celebration of Russian patriotism. Beethoven presented the folk-song theme thirteen times: eight times in a row, four times where the voices interrupt each other and one final rendition. But this banal, repetitive treatment of the theme was possibly satirical.[12] For a composer so magnificently skilled at developing his material the thirteen literal repetitions sounded suspiciously like a joke at the count's expense. And as if to emphasise the point, the Trio was repeated yet one more time later in the movement, supplying a further thirteen statements of the folk song.

After we finished the movement Fay and Harry walked up to the stage. This was only the second time I had met Harry, a Texas oil-company executive who had retired in Colorado, home of his earlier sporting triumphs. As quarterback of the Colorado School of Mines football team, he had led them to an undefeated season in 1939. Fay had been responsible for Harry's newly found interest in classical music.

'How much Bartók do you guys play?' Harry asked.

'A lot,' I said. 'He wrote six quartets and I have to learn them as quickly as possible so we can play the two-concert cycle. Maybe some day I'll make us play some English music.'

'It doesn't look very good for the instruments, the way you're hitting them: what was that snapping sound you made?'

Harry had noticed the Bartók pizzicato, a special technique where the player pulls the string up before letting go, causing it to snap against the fingerboard.

'Don't worry, we are more careful than it looks.' András looked pointedly at me. 'And we don't play too many Bartóks – it's a small percentage of the total.'

'That's good,' said Harry.

'How do you feel?' Fay asked. 'If you like them I would like to help with András and Karcsi's instruments.' She spoke as if merely offering us tickets to a football game. 'We met with Dean Daniel Sher today and he can arrange for us to loan the instruments to the university for your use.' Still in his first year as Dean of the College of Music, Daniel Sher continued the supportive atmosphere fostered by his predecessor, Robert Fink, and had already begun to expand our residency to include more teaching and a new concert series.

'You know how much Fay loves the Takács,' said Harry, 'and I can see you need some help, as we all need help sometimes – I could only come to Colorado thanks to full scholarships. I hope they work well for you.' He grinned. 'Just don't play too much Bartók.'

Jim Warren and Michael Remenyi joined us. 'It's a great time to invest in instruments,' Jim said. They made an effective team, Jim calm and articulate, Michael beaming with excitement. We were grateful that they had shown an interest in us at the beginning of our search, before we had definite funding. On the way out of the hall Jim whispered to me, 'Just hang on to the Milan Guadagnini for the time being. I have the feeling Fay wants to buy it for you – she just needs more time.'

Fay asked András to schedule a tennis match for the

following week and a concert at her house later in the autumn, the only obligations she asked from us in return for her generosity. She requested that we not acknowledge her in our concert programmes: a patron with no interest in display. While many concert promoters were adopting a cautious approach, waiting to see how the new formation evolved before offering us concert engagements, Fay had decided to buy instruments for Karcsi and András only a year after I had joined the quartet. We felt most fortunate to be the beneficiaries not only of Fay's philanthropy but also of her willingness to take a chance with us.

A cautious review of Beethoven's Opus 59 quartets was published in the *Allgemeine musikalische Zeitung* on 27 February 1807:

> Three new, very long and difficult violin quartets by Beethoven, dedicated to the Russian ambassador, Count Razumovsky, also attract the attention of all connoisseurs. They are deep in conception and marvellously worked out, but not universally comprehensible – with the possible exception of the third one in C major which cannot but appeal to intelligent lovers of music because of its originality, melody and harmonic power.[13]

The first players were less circumspect, distressed that the music did not behave as classical chamber music should. After the cellist Bernhard Romberg played the opening solo from the second movement of Opus 59, no. 1, he threw his music to the ground and stamped on it. What sort of sorry excuse for a tune was this? How insulting to give a cellist of his stature a banal rhythm that simply repeated a

B flat for four whole bars, the sort of thing anyone could tap out with a pencil!

The violinist Felix Radicati was bold enough to describe the new quartets in the composer's presence as 'not music'. Beethoven retorted, 'Oh, they are not for you, they are for a later age!'

Some of Beethoven's contemporaries came to his defence. In July 1810 E. T. A. Hoffmann, the same author whose story *The Nutcracker and the Mouse King* inspired Tchaikovsky's ballet, addressed contemporary criticism of Beethoven in an extensive review and analysis of his Fifth Symphony (composed between 1804 and 1808): 'It is customary to see in his works simply the products of a genius that, unconcerned with the form and selection of its ideas, gives itself over to its own fire, and to the momentary promptings of imagination.' But Hoffmann disagreed with this judgement, arguing that Beethoven successfully retained control of his diverse material. Just as when encountering a Shakespeare play, with familiarity would come increased comprehension of the structural unity of the work.[14]

In a later age Pozdnyshev, the protagonist of Leo Tolstoy's novella *Kreutzer Sonata* (published in 1889), described the frightening loss of control he experienced when listening to the first movement of another of Beethoven's middle-period works, the 'Kreutzer' Sonata for violin and piano (composed in 1803): the 'effect is neither to elevate nor to degrade but to excite. How can I explain it to you? Music makes me forget myself, my real situation. It transports me into a state that is not my natural one.' According to Pozd-nyshev, military marches, dance music and music for a religious service fulfilled a useful role, whereas a piece like the 'Kreutzer' Sonata, not confined to such a specific function, was bound to exert a harmful influence.[15]

Beethoven's middle-period compositions confounded expectations, taking those who encountered them to places they were not prepared to go and challenging assumptions about how music should affect them. As we played through the first movement of Opus 59, no. 2 in preparation for our Chicago concert, I could understand those first players and audiences who found these quartets disconcerting. Fast sections felt awkward to play, bowing arms jerked to and fro across strings while left-hand fingers became all too easily tangled up in intricate passagework. Restless flurries of semiquavers, jagged dynamic contrasts and abrupt pauses created a mood of breathless unease. I found it hard to remain relaxed enough to execute the difficult passages – the music was playing me, a fairground ride propelling me on many twists and turns before throwing me out the other end bruised and disoriented.

I asked Gábor how the first violin and viola could play better together when we were left alone near the beginning playing a string of semiquavers. 'Smoother string crossings if possible.' He coughed roughly, struggling to shake off a virus that had been bothering him throughout the summer. We should play with as seamless a technique as possible, minimising the distance between strings with our bowing arms, and moving our left-hand fingers as lightly as possible on the fingerboards.

To counterbalance the unruliness of the music we

concentrated on unifying our approach. The piece starts dramatically with two chords followed by a silence. To convey the ferocity of Beethoven's opening we would need to execute the chords in exactly the same manner as each other. By starting with bows on the string and using a pinching motion in our right-hand fingers – to make the bow bite and then release the string – we could initiate a more precise attack than if we all threw our bows from above the string. Although it was tempting to play these dramatic gestures with very fast bow speed, applying a slightly slower speed gave our bows a chance to pull a more full-bodied tone out of the instruments.

The following silence – one of several that fractured the opening music – needed to be played just as much as the music. We froze our positions before continuing. This opening is an extraordinary departure from Beethoven's previous quartets. Two chords. A silence. A short wisp of a *pianissimo* melody starting with the same notes as the opening chords. Another silence. And now a further shock. The melody is repeated a semitone higher, pulling the rug from underneath us by raising doubts about which key we were in.

The unprecedented sense of disruption right at the beginning of this piece must have contributed to the discomfort of its first listeners. Sonata form was the most common structure employed by composers of this period in the opening movement. From their experiences listening to the Opus 18 quartets, audiences would have expected Beethoven to lay out a well-proportioned opening melody of reasonable length which established the key. Opus 59, no. 1 begins with a much longer phrase than was typical, while the stops and starts of the second

'Razumovsky' quartet are even more disorienting.

During his first decade in Vienna Beethoven's improvisations on the piano had stunned his audiences. The conductor Ignaz von Seyfried offered a typical reaction:

> Now his playing tore along like a wildly foaming cataract, and the conjurer constrained his instrument to an utterance so forceful that the stoutest structure was scarcely able to withstand it.[16]

By 1805 Beethoven was infusing his string quartets, sonatas, concerti and symphonies with some of this same spirit of improvisation.

In a sonata-form movement the second main section, the development, is the place where audiences would have expected Beethoven to allow his imagination the greatest freedom: moving in and out of remote keys, making dynamic contrasts even more extreme – above all conveying the sense that the music had come far from its opening. The development sections in the first movements of the first two 'Razumovsky' quartets are much longer in proportion to the other sections than is the case in the Opus 18 quartets. Only in the third quartet of the Opus 59s, which I played in my audition with the Takács and which the contemporary reviewer conceded was the easiest to understand of the three, does the development section approach the compact scale of the earlier quartets.

Much of the excitement in the first-movement development section of Opus 59, no. 2 is generated by rhythmic opposition – the two violins pitting themselves against the viola and cello, the viola then changing allegiance to the violins as the music grows from *pianissimo* to a cataclysmic *fortissimo* arrival in C major – the very same key that tries to usurp E minor in the last movement. But even this outburst is no more than a passing drama; only seconds later we are plunged into yet another key. Immediately afterwards the music again retreats to *pianissimo*.

To control the cascades of fast notes that dominate the movement we practised with a metronome, learning when we tended to fall behind or rush forward. None of us liked relying on an autocratic mechanical beat but it was a useful referee in cases where one person thought we were rushing and another disagreed. We rehearsed a little below our eventual concert tempo, hearing more detail in the sometimes dense textures. By these means we hoped to create a stronger technical foundation for our performance. Paradoxically, in order to convey emotional instability in the music we worked to develop a greater level of control and confidence.

As we rehearsed sections repeatedly I worried that our performance would become too studied. How to convey the daring sense of digression in this music when the purpose of rehearsals seemed to be to build a secure sense that we knew exactly what was coming next?

'The surprise is there in the music,' said András. 'If we are secure it will sound convincing.'

'We can rehearse like crazy and then just enjoy, forget, in the concert.' Karcsi relished a sense of spontaneity onstage, sometimes instigating an exciting wave of forward momentum, taking the whole group along with him on a ride different from anything we had rehearsed.

'Each concert is different – the acoustic in each hall, amounts of sleep, how you feel onstage. You can't predict everything. It helps me to prepare the music carefully.'

Gábor showed me his part. The bowings and fingerings were written in meticulously, while different coloured pencils were used to highlight dynamics and phrase shapes. Sometimes Gábor had cut and pasted whole sections of the music to make an easier page turn or attached a third page to reduce the number of turns. Even these extra flaps were prepared in a precise manner, enough space left between the taped edges of the paper that the extra page could be smoothly closed at the end of a concert.

Gábor's attention to detail was an effective antidote to turbulent music or the unpredictabilities of a live performance. He took the most painstaking efforts to keep chaos at bay, arriving thirty minutes early to go through a rigorous warm-up routine before each rehearsal and swimming every day to train for the physical demands of a long tour. When I occasionally felt overwhelmed by the amount of new music I had to learn or a particularly gruelling travel schedule, he reassured me: 'There are three elements: your professional and personal life and your health. If two are going well, you can manage.'

Before the end of the breathless first movement of Opus 59, no. 2 a moment of relief comes for players and audience alike. The ferocious bustle of semiquavers is banished and while the first violin and cello sustain long notes, the second violin and viola pass back and forth a motif derived from the opening theme, growing ever quieter:

In isolation the duet was unremarkable, but in the context of the relentless momentum and ever-changing emotions of the previous music Karcsi and Gábor's dialogue yearned for an escape to somewhere less antagonistic. The ability to communicate a transformation of musical character from intense activity to contemplative stillness was one of the things I admired most about my colleagues: while the music imposed physical changes – slower bowing arms and left-hand fingers – the character change was reflected most powerfully in their eyes. Previously they had looked around the group with razor-sharp alertness. Now they seemed to retreat, no longer maintaining visual contact but, judging from the way they responded to each other's melodic shapes, listening all the more carefully – two people withdrawing from a frenzied public scene to share a private sorrow.

In the quartets dedicated to Razumovsky Beethoven presented a vivid spectrum of emotions at times linked to his personal experience. 'Let your deafness be no more a secret – even in art,' he had written at the top of a sketch of the last movement of Opus 59, no. 3, but this was not the only autobiographical reference in the Opus 59 quartets. In one of the sketches for the slow movement to the first 'Razumovsky' quartet Beethoven wrote: 'A weeping willow tree onto the grave of my brother.'[17] Although not quite the tragic utterance it seemed – Beethoven's brother had not died, he had merely got married – the melancholy pronouncement may have been a commentary either on his relationship with his brother or a prophetic insight into relations with his new sister-in-law, with whom he would have many future difficulties.

Beethoven's middle-period works emerged both from

the despair brought on by the dramatic deterioration of his hearing and from the trauma precipitated by the Napoleonic Wars. By including two Russian folk songs in the Opus 59s, Beethoven connected his music not only with its Russian patron but also with the failure of the Russian and Austrian armies to contain Napoleon. Hoffmann was confident of Beethoven's 'absolute' authority over his material, but perhaps the composer's goal was to include such variety and intensity of emotion as to challenge structure and meaning – threatening them just as a personal crisis could disrupt emotional stability or a Napoleonic army wreak havoc on a way of life. Viewed in this light the troubled reactions of the first unsuspecting players and audiences were perhaps more significant than those of connoisseurs who after repeated study and listening might congratulate themselves on recognising melodies, harmonies and structure – displaying none of the shock and disorientation of their less seasoned companions.

Beethoven had described the 'Razumovsky' quartets as music 'for a later age', but would never have wished them to be considered comfortably familiar repertoire, programmed to balance more radical, indigestible music elsewhere in a concert. While I had no wish to repeat the mistake I had made at the end of Opus 59, no. 2 during the concert in Cuernavaca, the experience at least connected me to the shock felt by some of Beethoven's contemporaries. The 'Razumovsky' quartets would never satisfy those listeners who required music merely to serve a narrowly defined function, whether it be to enhance worship, to inspire dance, to regulate the act of marching or simply to amuse. As I grappled with Opus 59, no. 2 I found the notion that this music might be intended to disturb strangely reassuring. It was legitimate to feel a little intimidated, to be destabilised as if by a traumatic, life-changing event.

As Beethoven worked on the Opus 59 quartets in 1806, Razumovsky's position as ambassador became precarious. It is not clear what precipitated this situation, but Razumovsky's unwavering anti-Napoleon stance probably brought him into conflict with an unpredictable Tsar who vacillated in his attitude to his French counterpart, uncertain if he was a genius or the devil. Razumovsky had perceived Napoleon's self-coronation as Emperor in 1804 as an affront to the natural social order: 'Who would have thought that an adventurer, raised at the expense of the Bourbons, would then set himself in their place and demand honours for himself . . . such as even the descendants of one of the oldest dynasties in Europe had never dared pretend to.'[18]

In addition to political differences with Razumovsky, Tsar Alexander may have subscribed to the view later expressed by German historian Johann Heinrich Schnitzler: 'Razumovsky lived in Vienna like a prince, encouraging art and science, surrounded by a luxurious library and other collections and admired and envied by all; what advantages accrued from all this to Russian affairs is another question.'[19] This view was not universally shared. Razumovsky had acquired supporters who valued his tact, intelligence and consistent resistance to Napoleon. In 1806, the diplomat Robert Adair was sent to Vienna by the English government to strengthen the alliance of countries against France. The foreign secretary Charles James Fox advised Adair, if 'Razoumowski be still in Vienna, to cultivate his friendship, and show him every proof of entire confidence'.[20]

Magnificently situated in his new palace, Razumovsky had no intention of leaving Vienna, even when a new ambassador, Ernst Graf von Stackelberg, was eventually sent there in 1810. Despite the tenuous nature of his situation, the count continued to exert his influence during this period. After Alexander signed the Treaty of Tilsit in 1807, making peace with Napoleon, Razumovsky's palace gained a reputation as a hotbed of anti-Napoleonic sentiment. The count threw frequent parties where gambling and music were the backdrop for political debate. In addition to his diplomatic activities, the count continued to focus on his musical interests and indulge his passion as a collector. His palace housed paintings by Rubens, Rembrandt and Van Dyck, while the library boasted over seven thousand manuscripts.

There is no record of Razumovsky's reaction to the quartets he commissioned, but during the next years the count would demonstrate his unwavering support for Beethoven. In 1808, filling the vacuum created by Prince Lichnowsky's rift with the composer, he asked Ignaz Schuppanzigh to form a string quartet to be in residence at his palace. Schuppanzigh chose the violist Franz Weiss and the cellist Joseph Linke. Although Razumovsky had perhaps imagined himself as the regular second violinist in the group, he ceded his position to Schuppanzigh's young pupil, Joseph Mayseder. Rehearsals of this difficult music were probably less constrained when the talented pupil replaced his employer in the second-violin chair.

It is no coincidence that the emergence of the first documented professional string quartet in Vienna occurred shortly after the composition of Beethoven's new string quartets. The technical and musical challenges that so frustrated their first players and audiences also created the need for a more professional approach to chamber music. By appointing a string quartet in residence at his palace Razumovsky responded to these demands. His employment of the quartet continued and formalised the tradition of chamber music in the homes of Beethoven's patrons while providing Beethoven with a wonderful opportunity to work with the musicians on his new music. In addition to the Opus 59 quartets, the Schuppanzigh Quartet would give the first performances of Beethoven's next quartets, Opus 74 and Opus 95.

According to Ignaz von Seyfried, this was an idyllic time for Beethoven:

> It is well known that Beethoven was as much at home in the Razumovsky establishment as a hen in her coop. Everything he wrote was taken warm from the nest and tried out in the frying pan. Every note was played precisely as he wanted it played, with such devotion, such love, such obedience, such piety as could be inspired only by a passionate admiration of his great genius.[21]

If this seems a suspiciously rosy portrayal of relations between the demanding composer and the sometimes bemused performers of his newest music, Beethoven would certainly have appreciated the amount of rehearsal time available. With Napoleon continuing to create turmoil throughout Europe, invading Vienna for a second time in 1809, the musicians had reason to be grateful for stable employment.

In October 1994, a week before our concert at the University of Chicago, we turned our attention to the slow movement of Opus 59, no. 2. According to Beethoven's piano student Carl Czerny, Beethoven was inspired to write this ethereal music, composed in the key of E major, 'when contemplating the starry sky and thinking of the music of the spheres'.[22] Each key brings out different tonal characteristics in a good instrument: E major teased a particularly gleaming sound from the Milan Guadagnini. As a result of Fay's recent miraculous decision to buy the violin for my use I could now revel in exploring its tonal possibilities, secure in the knowledge that I would not have to return it to Jim Warren.

The *Molto adagio* was one of the few string quartet movements I remembered hearing in a concert as a teenager, performed by the Allegri Quartet in the Guildhall in Cambridge. Several minutes into the slow movement the first violinist, Peter Carter, played a simple rising scale while the other three parts held a chord underneath. He climbed higher and higher and held one note a little longer than the others, as if reluctant to leave it, before beginning to descend. The chord enhanced the beauty of the line: certain pitches in the violin part harmonised with the chord while other dissonant notes rubbed against it creating a bitter-sweet effect. As I practised the same passage in my Boulder apartment twelve years later I tried to emulate Peter Carter's serene playing. But without the other parts my line was just an E major scale. Too often a bumpy bow change or left-hand shift halted me in mid-phrase. Czerny's anecdote about the stars and my memory of Peter Carter's sublime playing prompted greater dissatisfaction with my own efforts. I found it hard to create an appropriately ethereal mood on demand.

Beethoven utilised E major to set texts relating to the

stars in two vocal works. In the aria 'Komm Hoffnung' from his opera *Fidelio*, completed in its original version in 1805, Leonore disguised as the boy Fidelio visits a jail where she suspects her husband Florestan is being detained as a political prisoner. After overhearing the prison governor's plans to kill her husband, she sings: 'Abominable one! Where are you hurrying? / What are you planning in wild anger?' The music moves into E major as she pleads:

> Come hope, let the last star
> Not pale from fatigue!
> Light up my goal, be it ever so distant,
> Love will reach it.

In 1820 Beethoven would again link E major to the stars in his setting of Heinrich Goeble's poem 'Abendlied unterm gestirnten Himmel' ('Evening song under the starry sky', WoO 150). A premonition of mortality was relieved by the thought:

> Soon I will have reached my goal,
> Soon I will have ascended up to you.
> I will soon harvest at God's throne
> the lovely reward of my sorrows.

I found the idea of Leonore's new-found hope a more helpful image, love eventually triumphing over political oppression in an opera whose first performances had been in front of the officers of Napoleon's occupying army. An emphasis on hope rather than loss resonated with my own circumstances: Fay's purchase of a violin for me was the latest instalment of my adventure with the Takács and, only one year after my move to Boulder to join the quartet, I was thoroughly caught up in the exhilaration of new opportunities.

This movement could not have started more differently from the first movement: instead of two abrupt chords played by the whole group I began quietly, alone. One by one each instrument crept in – Karcsi, Gábor and finally András until we all played a chorale.

Beethoven's instruction, *Si tratta questo pezzo con molto di sentimento* ('this piece is to be played with great feeling'), was another indication of his wish to heighten personal expression in the 'Razumovsky' quartets: the instruction added yet more responsibility to play with depth and sincerity of feeling and did nothing to relax my muscles as I attempted the delicate solo entrance in rehearsal, my bow bouncing a couple of times on the string before slipping toward the fingerboard, like a stone briefly skimming the surface before disappearing into murky water.

'Try breathing out before you play so you can sink into it,' András suggested. Holding my breath created muscular tension elsewhere, making it harder to control my bow.

After the ferocious pace of rhythmic, harmonic and dynamic changes in the previous movement, here the music was stripped down to its bare essentials – simple chords moving just fast enough to prevent stasis. After the first phrase Gábor stopped. 'I think this feels too slow.' The difference between awe-struck wonder and somnolence was difficult to negotiate.

'Let's play more first,' said Karcsi. 'It's such a long movement.'

'Ed, you don't need to lead every note change with your

body language: that makes it too vertical. Try thinking in longer phrases,' András continued.

'Could we just try it a bit faster?' I asked.

'Let's play and not talk too much.' Karcsi raised his bow to the string purposefully.

We tried again. After roughly fifteen seconds I thought we sounded out of tune. When playing with a piano intonation is a less controversial issue; string players simply have to tune to the pre-ordained pitches. However in a string quartet there were no absolutes to rely on; the position of each note could be argued. We tried as much as possible to tune to the bass but this meant that András' tuning came under the closest scrutiny.

'Can you play that B a bit higher?' I asked.

'I could but I think you should bring your G sharp a bit lower. It's the third in the chord and that usually sounds too high.'

'It will be easier the more we play,' said Karcsi.

We began once again but I had too many questions to enjoy playing. Should we aim for an airy, floated sound, or something darker? How much vibrato to use and of what sort? Each of us was doing something different.

We reached a new theme in the cello and viola. To my ears András exaggerated the rhythm, creating a jerky, angular effect. 'That sounds too military, not singing enough.'

'That's what I want. A general, proud of beating Napoleon.'

'Are you sure?' asked Karcsi. 'Isn't it more noble?'

'That is noble.'

'Anyway, Napoleon was beating everyone else,' I chipped in.

Gábor began to say something, but his persistent cough intervened. He left the room to get a glass of water.

Receiving too much advice from colleagues about a carefully considered solo could be frustrating. We had reached one of those low points that occur in a rehearsal where despite everyone's earnest desire to make progress, the relentless illumination of technical and musical challenges causes paralysis and frustration. When Gábor returned we were more open to Karcsi's idea of playing the movement through. 'The first person to stop has to buy the others a drink,' he warned mischievously. After rehearsing in this manner the financial penalty seemed less of a deterrent than the necessity of spending further time in each other's company.

Relieved of all responsibility to improve our playing by talking I focused on reacting to what I heard around me. Now that I understood the reasoning behind András' approach to the general's melody I enjoyed its stately character; perhaps in response to our criticisms he had also made the rhythm a little less aggressive. I liked this aspect of rehearsing – allowing the criticisms of others to influence our playing more than we might concede during initial discussion. The articulation of ideas was often enough to move an interpretation forward even if differences were not resolved verbally.

Playing a longer section forced us to concentrate on taking melodies over from each other as smoothly as possible instead of stopping to suggest how each person could improve his rendition. We tried to match our timbres and phrase shapes while observing facial expressions and body language – clues as to what each person was trying to express. I loved the way Gábor played a repeated rhythm with a quietly insistent bow-stroke, seeming at first to resist the dynamic instruction *mancando* (dying away), András' high cello melody emerging from the eventual capitulation in the viola part. In this slower music where *crescendi* and *diminuendi* were dynamic changes often spread over a longer period of time, yielding to a change too easily was less interesting dramatically than beginning it hesitantly, a transformation more engaging for having been initially delayed.

After music that was for the most part idyllic I was puzzled by a passage near the end of the piece where the opening chorale was restated, but this time *fortissimo* with additional accents in the middle of each bar, disrupting the shape of the melody. Was this a moment of ecstasy? Or an angry shattering of the idyll? The passage seemed to challenge the serene character of most of the movement, just as the pleading duet between Karcsi and Gábor at a similar point in the first movement had proposed an alternative to previous agitation, or the slow rendition of the folk song near the end of the first 'Razumovsky' quartet had briefly transformed the melody into its original melancholy character. However dominant the prevailing mood, it was as if Beethoven was guarding against too simple a characterisation, never allowing his audience to take for granted the emotional trajectory of the music.

Nonetheless, large sections of this slow movement required the greatest spirit of cooperation. I found it more helpful to think of the 'great feeling' that Beethoven asked for in terms of our attitudes to each other – 'this piece is to be played with gratitude and not accompanied by excessive discussion' would have been a more useful instruction. By concentrating on taking over and handing on the seamless melodic lines imagined by Beethoven, I hoped both to enjoy and to communicate the relief offered from the restlessness of the previous movement.

Unable to look at each other, we played because we could think of nothing else to do. There was a chance that we would still go to Chicago. We went through the motions of playing but 'we' had been irretrievably fractured by Gábor's news. The music provided no solace, its serenity as grating as the oblivious ridges of the Flatirons etched into a relentlessly blue sky. On the campus paths the imminent onset of autumn was cheerfully denied by runners and bikers decked out in aerodynamic gear, cardiovascular performances reaching new heights as they tuned ever more efficient bodies.

If the results of initial tests were confirmed the doctors estimated Gábor would live for between two and six more months, his lungs and bones invaded by cancer. After we finished rehearsing the *Molto adagio* Gábor drove home to his apartment, where he placed his carefully tended music in a filing cabinet and his viola in its case on a shelf, never to play it again.

Beethoven's music seemed irrelevant that day, as inappropriate as it had to some of its first players and listeners. Never mind the stars, Leonore, or an idyllic mountain scene: from now on I would associate this music with the terror in Gábor's eyes.

For a long time I had nurtured pleasant feelings of superiority about my vocation. If music tapped emotional states more powerfully than any other art form, I reasoned, I must therefore be more in touch with my feelings than most. But during the following months, while Gábor's condition deteriorated, music became something to hide behind, a way to evade emotion. Taking my violin out of its case, tuning the instrument, playing scales, études, keeping my fingers in shape, putting the violin away, going to rehearsal, opening the case again, rehearsing with Karcsi, András and substitute violists: all contributed to a flimsy framework designed for getting through the day. My preferred musical enterprise was Book I of Henry Schradieck's *The School of Violin-Technics: Exercises for Promoting Dexterity in the Various Positions*. This veritable Kama Sutra of left-hand violin technique could be played with as little feeling as possible, fingers executing the same monotonous drills over and over again with no danger of any unpredictable change of mood on the next page.

We cancelled the concert at the University of Chicago but, with the help of kind and expert violists Louise Williams, Erika Eckert and Zoltán Tóth, continued to honour some of our engagements. At times there was a perverse satisfaction in inhabiting the robust and high-spirited mood of a Haydn finale before bowing with assumed cheerfulness to acknowledge applause at the end of a performance. Who would have thought that giving a concert could be such an exercise in deception? I was grateful for and yet sometimes ashamed by the structure of concert days that provided shape and rhythm in the face of potentially derailing emotion. Although Gábor insisted that the quartet continue to rehearse and perform in his absence, at times it seemed heartless that the life of the quartet marched relentlessly on.

Now I appreciated continuities. When we returned to the Wigmore Hall, its director, William Lyne, welcomed us as usual and provided encouragement after the concert; it brought welcome familiarity and supportive joy to spend time with Peter and Diana Held and Adele Schottlander, loyal quartet friends who hosted us in their houses whenever we stayed in London. Christa Phelps, the quartet's general manager who since 1983 had played an immense role in shaping the quartet's career, was a reassuring presence, managing to conceal her distress and anxiety while she worked hard to maintain relationships with concert promoters understandably uncertain about the quartet's viability.

After a necessarily rapid search process – several concert promoters and local managers refused to guarantee future engagements until we hired a new full-time violist – we found ourselves in February 1995 back at Fay's house with our new viola player, Roger Tapping, whom I had first seen perform when he was a student at Cambridge University. With years of chamber music experience as a member of the Raphael Ensemble and Allegri Quartet, Roger was immediately a steadying influence, his intense focus in concerts complementing an amiable and compassionate presence offstage. After we had performed in Fay's living room she said to him with a wry smile, 'I'm pleased to hear that you already have such a nice-sounding viola.' Two years later, when Roger found a powerful Amati viola that worked better with the other instruments in the quartet, he would write to Fay asking if she might consider completing her string quartet of instruments. She agreed to purchase the Amati, commenting with characteristic brevity when she next saw him, 'Good letter.'

Even as Gábor grappled with different treatment options and depleted energy, he invited Roger to his apartment, eager to pass on any helpful information about his years in the Takács and to reassure himself about the future of the quartet. At our Boulder concerts Gábor hovered backstage, keen to hear the quartet in its new formation but worried that his cough might disturb the audience. After one such concert, anxious to help in any way he could, he showed me a place in the score where he suggested we could better match our bow-strokes. For nearly twenty years he had dedicated himself to the Takács, contributing a crucial element to their early successes, weathering the group's exciting yet wrenching move to Boulder from Budapest, and helping me both socially and musically to become one of the quartet. The last time I saw him he quickly changed the subject from his own state. 'I really like Roger,' he said with a smile. 'The quartet's going to be okay.'

Gábor died on 7 July 1995, seven months after his first diagnosis.

The first time we performed Opus 59, no. 2 after his death I was surprised to find myself in the company of music that was, if not exactly an old friend, at least a companion whose eccentricities were reassuringly familiar. Less daunted by the turbulent emotion of the first movement, I launched myself at both the first opening chords and the cataclysmic C major climax in the development section. What was there now to scare me in a piece of music, compared with the loss we had suffered? When we came to the breakneck conclusion to the whole piece I was no longer frightened of losing my place: a changed perspective had given me the courage the music demanded. In the *Molto adagio* I felt the irony of Roger's *mancando* viola line, dying away as instructed by the composer and yet offering the tentative beginning of a musical line between past and future – a way both to grieve and to begin to cope with our loss.

*

My anger towards the *Molto adagio* when we last played it with Gábor connected me to the experiences of those who first encountered the Opus 59s and had been in their own ways initially disappointed or outraged by music from which they required something different. But whereas I railed against jarring serenity so unsuited to our situation, those listeners who objected to Beethoven's middle style did so because the music was *too* traumatic – full of bizarre and seemingly lawless contrasts that induced unpredictable feelings. Our common discomfort was caused by expecting this music to fulfil too narrow a function, wishing it to affirm rather than challenge an emotional state.

Although the Opus 59 quartets would soon come to be better appreciated by those players and audiences willing to give them a second chance, a review in the *Allgemeine musikalische Zeitung* of Beethoven's next quartet, Opus 74, composed in 1809, expressed lingering reservations about his compositional evolution. Writing in 1811, the reviewer bemoaned the fact that Beethoven had not continued in the pleasing vein of the Opus 18s, seeing this latest quartet as an unfortunate continuation of excesses prevalent in the 'Razumovsky' quartets. A promising slow introduction, for example, lost its way in 'an unnecessary confusion of dissonances', while the third movement took the audience 'into the midst of the war-like dances of a wild nation'. The piece had been composed under trying circumstances, Beethoven's compositional routine disrupted by Napoleon's invasion of Vienna in July 1809. 'What a destructive, disorderly life I see and hear around me, nothing but drums, cannons and human misery in every form.'[23] But for the reviewer of Opus 74, a string quartet had no business reflecting such turmoil or misery: instead of remembering the dead or conveying despair 'it should cheer our minds with its soft pleasing play of fantasy'.[24]

Anyone hoping to have the mind cheered by Beethoven's next string quartet, Opus 95, would have been instantly discouraged by its title, *Quartetto serioso*. Beethoven composed this uncompromisingly terse and intense work in 1810. Although it was performed in Vienna in May 1814, Beethoven later warned the English musician Sir George Smart that the quartet was intended for a select audience of connoisseurs and should not be performed in a public setting.[25] It would be fourteen years until Beethoven returned to his string quartet project, and when he did so his continued innovations of form and emotional content would demand still more of audiences whose approval he nonetheless desired.

In 1813 Beethoven answered the detractors of his recent compositions by proving himself more than capable of delivering a crowd-pleaser when the occasion required. Following the Duke of Wellington's victory over the French army at Vittoria, Spain, on 21 June of that year, Johann Nepomuk Maelzel, an inventor of unusual musical instruments, had approached Beethoven with the idea of composing a piece for his versatile panharmonicon, which could imitate many instruments and sounds including cannon shots and gunfire. Maelzel suggested including 'God Save the King' as a suitable recognition of the duke's victory. The piece was entitled *Wellington's Victory at Vittoria*, or the *Battle Symphony*. As with the inclusion of Russian folk songs in Razumovsky's quartets seven years earlier, Beethoven accomplished the assignment with panache, appearing to derive considerable satisfaction from writing music for a particular purpose.[26] In case the audience should have any difficulty navigating the structure of the piece, Beethoven supplied the five sections with titles: British Entrance – French Entrance – Battle Allegro – March – Victory.

The *Battle Symphony* was enthusiastically received in December 1813. From two concerts 4006 florins were raised to help wounded Austrian and Bavarian soldiers. Eager to capitalise on the piece's popularity, Beethoven planned several more performances early in 1814 for his own financial gain. All these performances were given in the huge Redoutensaal in the Imperial Palace in Vienna. Beethoven's personal assistant, Anton Schindler, reported that, 'This hall afforded an opportunity to put into execution for the first time the many subtleties written into the *Battle Symphony*. From the long corridors and opposed rooms one could hear the enemy armies advance towards each other, creating a stunning illusion of the battle.'[27]

Subtleties indeed. On 29 November 1814, Tsar Alexander, the Empress of Russia, the King of Prussia, the Prince of Sicily and other members of royalty joined an audience of around three thousand in the Redoutensaal for a grand concert in Beethoven's honour. The Congress of Vienna had been in full swing for two months, featuring an extravaganza of parties, balls, romantic intrigues, banquets, concerts, theatre performances, sleigh rides and hunting parties. Thousands of people had travelled to Vienna to witness the spectacle of Europe's leaders celebrating the end of Napoleon's rule. The *Battle Symphony* was again greeted with enthusiastic applause, its unsuspecting audience unaware that only three months later Napoleon would escape his confinement on the island of Elba and resume hostilities.

Throughout the Congress, Beethoven was treated as a celebrity, doubtless to the immense satisfaction of his patrons. Prince Lichnowsky had died in April 1814 but according to Beethoven's personal assistant Anton Schindler, Count Razumovsky presented Beethoven to the monarchs of Europe.[28] By the end of the year Beethoven had received such generous gifts from many of them that he was able to invest some of his capital in Austrian bank shares.[29]

Beethoven's success was probably almost as gratifying to his loyal patron as was the vindication of Razumovsky's anti-Napoleonic stance. Razumovsky's position at the Congress was so prominent that one commentator continued to call him the Russian ambassador (a post now held by von Stackelberg):

> The Razumovsky Palace constituted one of the sights of Vienna . . . Several times since the opening of the Congress, Emperor Alexander had borrowed it of his ambassador. It was in these vast apartments that he had given some of the fêtes rivaling in pomp and splendour those of the Austrian Court; it was at the Razumovsky Palace that he had gathered around a table of seven hundred . . . all the political celebrities of Europe.[30]

His social successes were some compensation to Razumovsky for the difficulties inherent in representing Tsar Alexander. Despite the many parties Razumovsky held at his palace, his social acumen could not disguise the fact that amongst the assembled delegates Tsar Alexander was viewed with distrust. As soon as he arrived in Vienna Alexander proposed that he be made king of an expanded

Poland, the extra lands to be taken from Prussia and Austria. Alexander further demonstrated his diplomatic skills by throwing his sword onto a table and demanding a duel with the Austrian minister, Prince Klemens von Metternich. The representative of defeated France, Charles Maurice de Talleyrand, seized the opportunity to become one of the most influential diplomats in Vienna, arguing that it was Russia rather than France that represented the greatest threat to European stability. On 3 January 1815 Britain, Austria and France would sign a secret defensive alliance against Russia and Prussia.

When seven hundred guests had assembled at the Razumovsky Palace four days earlier on the evening of 30 December 1814, animosities were put aside, but in the early hours of the morning of 31 December, after the guests had departed, catastrophe struck. In order to accommodate the many revellers the count had added an additional temporary room to his edifice, one heated by a flue connecting it to the main palace. The French hot-air heating system caused the ducts in the walls to become so hot that the wooden structure burst into flames. The fire spread quickly into the main rooms of the palace, as a contemporary observer recalled:

> Soon, there was not a window in the new Palace that did not emit smoke or flames, the copper roof glowed a fiery red. This most valuable part of the count's residence, with its priceless collections, its exclusive library, and all the other treasures, was hopelessly lost.[31]

Word spread of the disaster and the Viennese police had to push back the crowds, terrified but exhilarated by the dramatic spectacle. Razumovsky's servants stayed as long as they could in the palace, throwing clothes, silverware, paintings, mirrors and books from the upper storeys. Many of these broke on impact, were ruined in the muddy mess created by water to fight the fire, or were removed by looters. Two chimney sweeps, motivated by the promise of a reward for retrieving valuable documents, fell to their death as the intense heat blew the copper sheeting off the roof.

Although Razumovsky began to rebuild the palace with the help of a loan from Tsar Alexander, his debts quickly became unmanageable. Unable any longer to support the musicians of the Schuppanzigh Quartet, the count soon disbanded the group. Despite his own financial hardship the count granted the musicians pensions, his last generous gesture as a patron of the arts. In November 1815, Alexander awarded the title of Prince to Razumovsky in recognition of his services during the Congress of Vienna.

In 1823, Ignaz Schuppanzigh returned to Vienna after a seven-year absence in St Petersburg, re-established his friendship with Beethoven and re-formed his quartet, violinist Karl Holz replacing Mayseder in the second-violin chair. Was there an affectionate reunion between the quartet musicians and their former patron? In the conversation books people used to communicate with Beethoven in the latter years of his life, there are brief mentions of Razumovsky – who was often travelling. He had ceased to pay the cellist Josef Linke's pension after only five years,[32] while Schuppanzigh also received his pension irregularly, according to Karl Holz who explained 'that it's not due to a lack of willingness to pay but that he probably has no money at the moment, as is often the case'.[33] There seems to have been little in the way of communication between Beethoven and his old patron, Beethoven's nephew merely reporting on one occasion to his uncle that Razumovsky was back in town 'but without money'.[34]

Razumovsky died in 1836. His sister-in-law from his second marriage, Countess Lulu von Thürheim, lived in the palace during his last years and kept a journal. In the summer of 1835 Lulu was 'at the side of a magnificent fishpond in his park and reading a book'. She heard Razumovsky's voice, turned to see him sitting in his wheelchair at the end of a terrace and feared that he would sense her distress at his condition: 'There were at that time so many sorrowful thoughts that we had shared between us and that nonetheless had no words for expression!'[35]

Would the prince have found any solace in the string quartets he commissioned, works that express such a broad range of emotions, including the sense of disorientation and emotional fracture that some listeners thought had no rightful place in a piece of music? Some years ago, in 2009, I walked back and forth along Razumovskygasse searching for the palace. Behind iron railings and surrounded by apartments and office buildings stood the only possible contender, dilapidated but recognisable. A disused and neglected anachronism, it gave no hint of its former glory.

And yet on a grey afternoon a few years later in February 2015 I was astonished to observe a transformation to the palace, immediately obvious from its freshly painted neoclassical façade. Two private art collectors had bought the palace and commissioned the Austrian architect Baar-Baarenfels to convert it into an art foundation and private residence. The ground floor had been turned into gallery space while the upper level was now a penthouse apartment surrounded by terraces with views of the gardens and surrounding buildings. Always an admirer of innovation, Razumovsky would have enjoyed the sophisticated system of sun-protection fins to offer solar control, although he would doubtless have interrogated the architects about the soundness of the new air-circulation system. After two hundred years, although it was still an unlikely venue for a G8 summit, some aspects of the palace's original function had been restored.

In the centre of Vienna later that evening, just over two hundred years after his palace had burned, Razumovsky would have been gratified to see some four hundred people coming together to hear a performance of the first of the Opus 59 quartets – even if the music's scale and extremes of emotional contrast (at least in this particular rendition) were not consistently to the taste of one audience member sitting in the front row, who while broadly smiling at the livelier sections of the opening movements could be seen halfway through the expansive slow movement inspecting his watch and communicating the fruits of his research to his female companion. 'A weeping willow tree onto the grave of my brother' might have been the inscription on one of Beethoven's sketches for the movement, but for this patron the *Adagio molto* had perhaps provided a little too much prolonged sorrow for one evening.

4

Re-creation: Opus 127

An imaginative lighting designer could not have chosen a better place in Schubert's 'Death and the Maiden' string quartet for a power cut. Schubert first explored the struggle between Death and a terrified maiden in his earlier song of the same name. He returned to the subject with the quartet in 1824, when he was already suffering from the illness that probably killed him four years later and when Beethoven was just embarking on his last string quartets. In Schubert's string quartet the maiden's final capitulation is conveyed towards the end of the slow movement by a slowing pulse in the viola part:

As Roger reached the end of his faltering line, the lights went out in the living room of Sasha and Thais Mark's house near the National Cathedral in Washington DC. In April 2000, thirty of Sasha's friends and colleagues had paid a generous admission fee to attend a house concert to help the Takács raise funds for our project to record the Beethoven quartets. If we had been plunged into darkness thirty seconds earlier during a more tumultuous and rhythmically complex section, the music would quickly have ground to a halt, but the serene chorale that concluded the movement was easy to remember – simple chords played in a uniform rhythm.

Deprivation heightened awareness. Although visual communication with each other and our audience was briefly removed, the timing of the power cut created a stronger musical link between players and audience, darkness intensifying the disembodied quality of the music and for a moment freeing the performance from the trappings of a specific time and place.

Whenever we began a recording session I wondered how to compensate for the lack of immediacy inherent in the medium. The process of recording a CD would thoroughly detach us from our audience, the end result electronically conveyed in the privacy of homes or cars at least a year later and many miles from the recording venue. But if the loss of sight at a house concert could enhance a listening experience, perhaps that could also hold true for a CD. Physical gyrations during a concert could detract from the music: one disgruntled audience member had written to our general manager in London complaining that the wildly swinging feet of the first violinist had ruined her enjoyment of our performance. While urging that I get my distracting habit under control, she also warned that she would boycott our concerts until we sent her a free CD. At least I wasn't the only violinist to provoke such a complaint. Commenting on the chamber music concerts that he heard in 1810, the musician Friedrich Reichardt had appreciated many aspects of Ignaz Schuppanzigh's playing, 'though he disturbed me often with his accursed fashion, generally introduced here, of beating time with his foot'.[1]

Stamping feet, noisy page turns, impromptu string tuning and the rubbing of brows with sodden handkerchiefs could be as distracting as open-mouthed explosions of phlegm in a resonant concert hall on a February evening.

In theory a pristine listening environment might aid focused listening. For our subscribers in DC, hearing our Beethoven CDs could perhaps provide the additional satisfaction of knowing that their generosity had facilitated the project – as long as they approved of the results.

The turn of the century was a questionable time to consider recording yet another cycle of Beethoven quartets to add to the wonderful interpretations by the Amadeus, Hungarian, Budapest, Alban Berg, Cleveland, Tokyo, Guarneri, Juilliard and Emerson Quartets, to name just a few. As CDs replaced vinyl records in the early 1990s, record companies flooded the market with new recordings of standard repertoire, but CD sales failed to recoup production costs. The profit margins of classical labels, often owned by larger corporate entities, came under closer scrutiny as executives sought to simplify their businesses. In September 1997, the twenty sound producers, engineers and drivers who comprised Decca's full-time production staff were made redundant, their parent company Polygram planning to save money by employing engineers and producers on a freelance basis. In 1998 Seagram, an alcohol-distilling company, acquired Polygram and warned of more redundancies. Fearing for the future of less profitable projects such as string quartet recordings, Evans Mirageas, in charge of Artists and Repertoire at Decca, pushed through a contract for a Takács Beethoven cycle – one of his last actions before he decided to leave the company.

This was the first time that we had been asked to finance any of the production expenses associated with a recording. Decca paid for the first two of seven sessions – enough to complete the Opus 59s and Opus 74, which we finished recording in 2001 – but in order to record the Opus 18s,

Opus 95 and the late quartets we would have to cover the costs of hotel rooms, hall rental and fees for a sound engineer and producer, which we estimated would add up to almost $100,000. Although the new financial arrangements seemed a daunting obstacle, as soon as we identified supporters willing to help us we discovered some benefits. Financing almost two-thirds of the costs gave us more control over the whole project. We were able to select our preferred venue, allot more time for each recording session and choose our two most important partners: the producer and the sound engineer.[2]

To some extent the producer of a music recording has a similar role to the director of a play, guiding the performers through each session and helping shape performances. But whereas a theatre director may choose actors to facilitate his vision for a play, a good chamber music producer's primary role is to help musicians realise their own interpretations of the music. The sound engineer performs the equally vital role of providing the recording equipment and mixing the sound together. During a session the sound engineer enables not only the recording but also the playbacks during which musicians retreat to the control room to evaluate their work.

For the Beethoven recordings we asked the highly regarded producer Andrew Keener to work with us – our violist, Roger Tapping, had previously loved working with Andrew and our trusted producer at Decca had recently changed careers. The sound engineer was Simon Eadon, one of several excellent engineers whom we had worked with at Decca and who now ran his own company. To take further advantage of our new-found freedom we gave ourselves more time to record each disc. Most recording companies budgeted three days to make a CD containing between sixty and eighty minutes of music. For the Beethoven cycle we allowed ourselves a generous five days per disc and chose as our venue St George's Brandon Hill, a decommissioned church near Bristol University well known for the warmth of its acoustics.

As a result of Sasha Mark's house concerts and similar initiatives by friends and supporters in Boulder, we were able to record the Opus 18s in 2002. In May 2004, having raised the funds we needed to finish the cycle, we prepared to return to Bristol to record the first of Beethoven's late quartets, Opus 127.[3]

During the ten years since Roger had joined the quartet we had gradually re-established a strong international concert schedule, guided by Christa Phelps and our new North American manager Seldy Cramer, who agreed to take us on in 1997. While frantically expanding our repertoire together there was little time to discuss the question we most frequently fielded: how did two Englishmen and two Hungarians work with each other? Musical disagreements were in fact just as likely to occur between Karcsi and András or Roger and myself as along national lines. Although the story of our quartet included loss and change, in the midst of it we put our heads down and concentrated on playing as well as we could, grateful for those many audience members and promoters willing to keep an open mind about the changes. If we did not often talk about Gábor Ormai, he was often on our minds. We threw ourselves into rehearsals and concerts as he would have wished us to, and had earlier dedicated our Decca recording of the Bartók quartets to him.

For reasons of expense and comfort we rented two

smaller cars rather than a large van. It must have been a relief for Karcsi and András to be able to talk in Hungarian, and I enjoyed Roger's company. Eight years my senior, he bridged the age-gap between me and the Hungarians and I came to think of him almost as an older brother, someone with a shared background on whom I could rely to trounce me at Scrabble, keep me up to date on English politics and provide sound personal and musical advice. One evening backstage after a bad day's travel, I doubted I could summon the energy to play a good concert. Roger's simple pronouncement was oddly reassuring: 'It's only 7.30; you don't need to feel in the mood for another twenty-five minutes.' Upon our arrival in Christchurch, New Zealand after a thirty-six-hour journey marred by missed flights and lost luggage we were met by the local manager who informed Roger that there had been a change of plan: he would have just enough time to unpack before teaching a keen viola student who had requested a last-minute lesson. Roger somehow transformed his wan features into an expression of eager anticipation.

'It's a good job that didn't happen to you, Ed,' said András, raising his eyebrows. 'You'd have blown up.'

Before joining us Roger had played in the English-based Allegri Quartet for six years, the same group whose Cambridge concert had made such an impression on me as a teenager, although that had been with a different violist. Roger brought great attention to the details of interpretation, encouraging me to linger over a surprising chord change where I might have been inclined to pass over it in too great a hurry, or tweaking the internal balance of the group to bring out a brief melodic shape in the second violin or cello part. Before the Opus 18 recordings Roger had researched a question of repeats in the third movements. While both the Minuet and Trio have repeat signs at the end of each section, the standard convention when playing the Minuet once again after the Trio (*da capo*) is to do so *without* the repeats. However, after consulting with other musicians and scholars Roger made the case that the short opening section of the Minuet should be repeated even after the Trio; otherwise it seemed too short in proportion to the rest of the piece. Unable to convert us to his point of view, Roger had designed one of his infamous April Fool's jokes, inventing a convincing review of our Opus 18 CDs which he faxed to our manager: the perceptive reviewer's enjoyment of other aspects of our interpretation had been regrettably ruined by the inexplicable omission of those first *da capo* repeats.

Sometimes I wondered if we spent too much time working on details, a particular issue in the late Beethoven quartets where the technical demands are ferocious and in some movements practically every bar is crammed with the composer's instructions. Playing sections much below tempo to work on tuning and blending our sounds was beneficial in small doses but liable to inspire a catatonic rehearsal atmosphere if overdone. As a result of performing several complete cycles together we learned how better to connect the contrasting sections of a long slow movement and which finales would require extra preparation so that we could deliver them with suitable sweep and energy towards the end of a two-hour concert.

Although we were thrilled when our Opp. 59 and 18 recordings won a Grammy and awards from Chamber Music America, the Japanese Recording Academy and *Gramophone* magazine, contemplating recording the late quartets was daunting: when compared with the earlier works the range of interpretative possibilities in the later quartets seemed vast. Beethoven had modestly declared his satisfaction with this music that he felt exhibited more fantasy than his previous compositions. The variety and sharp juxtaposition of moods were unprecedented, while Beethoven's increasingly complex writing raised fundamental questions for players about the relationships between the four voices – at times each individual part seemed so important that it could be hard to know how to balance the whole group.

The imminent recording session inspired a frantic review of all factors that I felt affected my sound. Discarded violin-string packets were strewn about my house and rejected strings presented a recurrent hazard to our vacuum cleaner as I tried out the latest innovations in string technology. The Thomastik Infelds were the latest brand to set my pulse racing and promised a dizzying number of alternatives: 'Red' for a warmer sound; 'Blue' for a brighter sound; each designed to complement the other so that one could use a combination of the two to bring out different tonal emphasis. Perhaps a brighter sound for the G and D and a warmer sound for the A would suit my violin the best? Or the opposite? Were the Infelds really an improvement on the dark power of the Vision Titanium Solos or the subtle warmth of the Pirastro Olives? It was a heady time not only for me but for my wife Beth and four-year-old son Sam, struggling to restrain their over-excitement at the dinner table as I explained the pros and cons of different types of strings and wondered whether or not to schedule a last-minute soundpost adjustment in London.

The small wooden post placed inside the violin

underneath the right side of the bridge transmits sound and vibration between the top and back of the instrument. Its position can be adjusted to bring out more bass or treble. Each instrument reacts differently to how the post is fitted: a tight post can make a violin more powerful and clearer, but if overdone it can choke the sound and risk cracking the wood. A looser post adjustment expertly executed by local luthier David Goodrich was ideally suited to Boulder's dry climate but sometimes produced a woollier sound in a more humid climate. While performing in London I often rushed off to another violin restorer, Mark Robinson, who inserted a metal tool into the violin and gently tightened the post by tapping it a millimetre to the left or right. I was grateful that Mark performed this delicate operation in front of me: in order to satisfy a particularly demanding client, one restorer had been known to retreat to an adjoining room where he made convincing tapping noises on a wall, after which he returned to the showroom to be congratulated on the miraculous tonal improvement.

At the dinner table I asked Beth and Sam if I should schedule an appointment for a soundpost adjustment in London or leave it to chance, hoping that the humidity in Bristol wouldn't be too severe this time. Sam gave the dilemma its deserved attention: 'Is there any more mac and cheese? When do you leave for tour, Dad?'

Focusing on the tangible aspects of violin sound masked a more serious anxiety. During our preparations for recording the earlier Beethoven quartets we had arrived at a relatively clear sense of what musical characters and tempi we would employ for the recordings, but after several years of performing Opus 127 my views of how to play it continued to change from one day to the next. Whereas concert performances could be tweaked from night to night to try out a different character or tempo, a recording claimed to be more definitive – a snapshot that ossified an interpretation, necessarily leaving out as much as it included. Were we ready to make the bold interpretative choices that would give our recording an individual stamp, distinguishing it from those recordings already available?

When Ignaz Schuppanzigh returned to Vienna from St Petersburg in April 1823 after a seven-year absence that had included concert tours in north Germany, Poland and Prussia, he planned to re-establish himself as Vienna's leading violinist and chamber music promoter, launching a new concert series featuring primarily the string quartets of Haydn, Mozart and Beethoven. Schuppanzigh had been closely involved in the first rehearsals and performances of Beethoven's previous quartets and urged him now to write a new one. Although the ambitious violinist expected Beethoven to entrust the first performance of any new quartet to him, Beethoven would turn out to be a capricious and hurtful partner.

Overwhelmed by the demands on his time and emotional energy, Beethoven managed his business dealings in the last years of his life in a chaotic and at times devious manner. Plagued by illness and weighed down by the financial responsibilities of supporting his nephew Karl – whose guardianship he had assumed in 1820 after a lengthy legal struggle with his sister-in-law – Beethoven exacerbated his situation by inefficient household management, maintaining two servants and sometimes more than one residence at once. He was so anxious to earmark savings to help Karl that he assumed debts in order to address his immediate financial needs, trying the patience of those who agreed to help him. In December 1820 the Viennese publisher Steiner complained of being short of money himself and begged the composer to repay a debt as soon as possible.

Although Beethoven still received an annuity from Viennese nobles, patronage was a lesser factor in sustaining a career in the 1820s than it had been when he was establishing his reputation in Vienna in the 1790s. His correspondence during this period was largely taken up with promoting and selling his work. In this evolving freelance environment he had assistance of often dubious worth from his brother Johann and personal assistant, Anton Schindler, both of whom attempted to represent Beethoven's interests – roles that later in the nineteenth century would begin to be assumed by impresarios or professional business managers.

In June 1822, Beethoven tried to interest the Leipzig publisher C. F. Peters in buying a new string quartet. He also hoped to persuade Peters to publish a complete edition of his music or, failing that, at least several of his unpublished works, including a Mass for chorus, soloists and orchestra (the *Missa solemnis*, Opus 123), some songs, four military marches and a piano sonata. For a new string quartet Beethoven proposed a fee of fifty ducats, a high fee for a single work. A month later he referred to the new quartet as not completely finished and explained to Peters that since he was most well paid for works of this sort, he would find it difficult to lower his fee.[4] In fact Beethoven would only begin serious work on the quartet that became Opus 127 nearly two years later, in May 1824, by which point he had not even decided on the key of the piece.[5]

A string quartet by Beethoven was low on Peters' list of

priorities. Having never paid that much for a string quartet before, the publisher feared he would make no profit.[6] He chose instead to print several 'beautiful, excellent' string quartets by other composers: Louis Spohr, the German violinist and conductor; Bernhard Romberg, the same cellist who had at first reacted so negatively to Opus 59, no. 1; and Pierre Rode, the French violinist known today primarily for his violin études. Peters would prefer Beethoven to compose a quartet for piano and strings.

> Then I ask, however, that it *not* be made *too difficult*, so that good dilettantes can enjoy playing it, for with the presently deteriorated tastes, one must lead amateurs back to better taste by means of works by *good* masters that are not too difficult, but rather more pleasant.[7]

By promoting the quartets of Spohr, Romberg and Rode, works neither too difficult to play nor too hard to understand, the judicious publisher hoped to educate the taste of the musical public.

Being spurned by Peters perhaps made Beethoven more appreciative of the interest shown by a new patron. In January 1823, he received fifty ducats as an advance payment for one of three quartets commissioned by Prince Nikolai Galitzin, an amateur violoncellist in St Petersburg who was also involved in the financing and first performances of the *Missa solemnis* (Beethoven would later also be paid the same amount by the publisher Schott for the publication rights to Opus 127).

For much of the next two years Beethoven was so occupied with the composition and first performances of the *Missa solemnis* and the Ninth Symphony that the new quartet project was pushed to one side. In January 1825, a hopeful Schuppanzigh, under the impression that Beethoven had promised him the first performance of Opus 127, advertised it as part of his upcoming concert series.[8] But Beethoven's brother Johann had simultaneously promised the rights to the first performance, which included a share of the profits from ticket sales, to the cellist in Schuppanzigh's quartet, Joseph Linke. Beethoven now tried to back out of his commitment to Schuppanzigh, supported by Johann and his nephew Karl, who worried that the size of Schuppanzigh's stomach was impeding his violin playing.[9] Schuppanzigh complained to Beethoven: 'This is a vexing business with the quartet . . . I wouldn't say anything about it, if it hadn't already been in the newspaper. I can't retract that.'[10]

The fact that Beethoven was favouring a cellist must have been doubly insulting to a first violinist accustomed to thinking of himself as the force behind any ensemble. If Linke were allowed to present the first performance, he might not even choose Schuppanzigh to participate, perhaps preferring one of the violinists who had benefitted from the illustrious leader's seven-year absence in St Petersburg. Schuppanzigh was already sensitive to being overlooked: hoping to gain regular employment he had applied the previous year for a teaching position, only to be rejected in favour of a twenty-five-year-old violinist.

Schuppanzigh's annoyance was effective: Beethoven allowed him to go ahead with the first performance of Opus 127, while Joseph Linke was given the first rights to the next quartet, Opus 132. Although Schuppanzigh sold tickets for a first performance to take place in February 1825, Beethoven completed Opus 127 too late for the concert and more than two years after Prince Galitzin had paid him for it.

When Beethoven delivered the parts to the musicians, a mere two weeks before the rescheduled first performance on 6 March 1825, he attached this cheerful document:

> Most Excellent Fellows!
>
> Each of you is receiving herewith his part. And each of you undertakes to do his duty and, what is more, pledges on his word of honour to acquit himself as well as possible, to distinguish himself and to vie in excellence with the others.
>
> Each of you who is participating in the said undertaking must sign this paper.[11]

The contract was signed by Beethoven and the four players who first tackled the piece – Schuppanzigh was joined by violinist Karl Holz, violist Franz Weiss and cellist Joseph Linke. Although musicians were accustomed to having to learn new music quickly, Beethoven's anxiety about the challenges of Opus 127 had perhaps motivated this contract urging the musicians to do their best.

For the remaining two years of his life, Beethoven would devote himself primarily to composing string quartets, completing Opus 132 and Opus 130 for Prince Galitzin, as well as two further quartets, Opp. 131 and 135.

In the control room beneath the hall at St George's in Bristol we assembled, anxious to acquit ourselves as well as possible. Our producer, Andrew Keener, sat next to the sound engineer, Simon Eadon, in front of a console, laptop and loudspeakers. For the initial sound-check we had recorded two contrasting musical excerpts and would now listen to them to help us judge the quality of sound and the balance between the four instruments. In order to reduce the variables, Simon had placed the chairs and microphones on the stage in the exact positions he had measured at the end of our previous recording session.

The technique of capturing sound electronically introduces more possibilities to feed the obsessive personality of a performer. The acoustic of the hall, the type of microphones and their placement, and the skill of the producer or sound engineer can all become convenient scapegoats for a player's dissatisfactions. Although canny microphone placement in a good acoustic can help achieve a great recorded sound, so too do the minute and subconscious adjustments made by the players in reaction to first hearing themselves over loudspeakers. In much the same way that stage actors accustomed to reaching the back row must modify their techniques under the microscopic scrutiny of a film camera, musicians trained to project to the back of a concert hall must adjust to the proximity of microphones. Bow articulations that translate into the clear beginnings of notes at the back of a hall may sound rough and scratchy when picked up at close quarters by a microphone. The brilliance of high violin notes may help carry them to the back of a concert hall but be too strident under the closer examination of the microphone.

In the first excerpt we recorded, taken from the opening movement of Opus 127, each part played against the others in ferocious counterpoint. The section was a good test of whether the four parts could be heard clearly.

'I'd like the same bite on the beginning of my notes as Ed.'

'Are you sure, András? The group balance is good: do

you really want to change that, just for the cello sound?' I asked. With five days of recording sessions ahead of us an early night seemed a greater priority to me than fussing around with microphone placement – I was always happy with the final sound mix that Andrew and Simon achieved.

'The sound's good overall; I just miss a bit of focus for my lower strings,' András said.

'The mix between us is nice,' said Roger. 'I wouldn't want the sound to be much more direct.'

'Try listening on the headphones,' suggested Andrew. Each control room has its own individual acoustics: with stone walls and a low arched ceiling, the faintly mould-scented control room at St George's didn't favour the bass.

'It's better but still not quite enough bite.'

In the late quartets, composed between 1824 and 1826, Beethoven experimented with a 'new type of voice-leading', as he would later describe it to a friend[12] – varying and expanding the way the four parts cooperated and argued with each other. Instead of his previously favoured method of sketching on one or two staves, from an early stage of working on Opus 127 Beethoven gave himself the additional space of four individual staves, emphasising the added independence of the parts. The increased autonomy of the voices could create problems of balance for the players and sound engineer – the second violin, viola and cello even more democratic partners than in the Opus 59 quartets. No wonder cellist Joseph Linke fancied starting his own concert series in competition with Schuppanzigh: why should the first violinist have all the fun?

'Are you sure you are playing as loudly as you usually do?' I asked András, wondering how hard it would be to find a table at a restaurant in the middle of Bristol on a Friday night. Perhaps room service would be a better option. My anxiety about the task ahead made me intolerant of differences of opinion.

'I don't want my sound to be more distant if we change the cello sound,' said Karcsi.

Andrew listened with complete concentration, gauging the temperature of the discussion and pondering how to achieve a solution; his cheerful, collaborative spirit set an example that I should try to emulate. 'Simon, do you think we could bring András' spot mic in a bit closer?' he asked. 'If we don't like it, we can always go back to this.'

Simon made an adjustment and we returned to the hall and recorded the passage again. Listening again we all admitted that the change was an improvement, András happier with the clarity of his lower notes and the rest of us relieved that this had been achieved with no detriment to anyone else.

We listened to the next recorded excerpt, the lyrical conclusion to the first movement, which would tell us more about the timbre of recorded sound. This was an example of Beethoven sustaining an unusually long melodic line shared between the instruments. Taking as his starting point the last gesture of the opening theme from the first movement, Beethoven began in the first violin:

then switched to the second violin, and on to the viola who expanded the fragment into a longer statement. The first violin took over again, then the second violin elaborated on

the idea so that what had started as a graceful way to tie up
a phrase became the main event:

It was as if a fragment of memory, at first tentatively
offered, now led to an extended reminiscence. Unlike the
first example we had recorded, where the four parts vied
with each other, this music required delicate cooperation.

To help sustain the melodic line Beethoven used an
unusual dynamic device. Just as a *crescendo* seemed to
reach an arrival point, a sudden drop to *piano* confounded
expectations – like an actor building suspense and then
dropping his voice to draw us in – before the story continued. After several *crescendi* the melody retreated, ending in a final whisper.

'Is there enough space around the sound?' Roger asked,
back in the control room.

'I think so,' said Andrew. 'I don't think we'd like it any
more resonant.'

Since CDs are usually heard in a small room or over
headphones, trying to reproduce the aural experience of an
audience member sitting in the middle of the church would
be unwise. The first time Andrew had worked with us, he
and Simon moved the microphones a little closer to us than
we had been accustomed to from previous sessions, aiming
to pick up more of the character of the individual instruments and a little less of the sound of the hall. They created
a microphone set-up that would capture some sense of the
resonance and warmth of St George's while nonetheless
retaining clarity.

'I think you can make more of the dynamic contrasts,' said Andrew, 'but that's for tomorrow.'

'Simon, András sounds great,' said Karcsi. 'I'll buy you a drink to turn that cello mic off tomorrow.'

'Maybe I never turned it on.'

Although we were certain that Simon was joking, subterfuge was sometimes effective. Another sound engineer once told us that a famous opera singer insisted on having two microphones in front of him, convinced that only in this arrangement could the essence of his sound be captured. His request was granted but the sound engineer turned on only one of the microphones. A harmonious session ensued. After many years of experience dealing with the fragile egos of musicians, Andrew and Simon had fine-tuned their approaches. Andrew took our comments seriously but knew when to make allowances for nerves or tiredness. Simon combined his quiet, authoritative expertise with humour, introducing well-timed puns of variable merit to lighten the mood. In his opinion, although the sound-check focused on microphone placement, fifty per cent of the improvement came from the instinctive adjustments the players made after listening back to themselves.

The success of the next days would depend largely on our ability to make such adjustments. Over the loudspeakers there had been nothing of the whispered quality I desired about my tone at the end of the first movement: the sound was too present to create a sense of reminiscence as the opening tune was first extended and then dissolved into silence. While the proximity of microphones could enhance clarity, it could also encourage more daring experiments with the quietest spectrum of dynamics. When we came back the next morning I would try playing this section closer to the fingerboard with a faster bow speed, hopefully making a floated, fragile sound to convey a stronger musical character: regret for a lost melody.

Later that evening I regretted my choice of reading material. Beethoven had stayed away from the first performance of Opus 127 on 6 March 1825, perhaps fearing that his deafness would ruin his enjoyment or perhaps from a sense of foreboding. In his report on the concert to his uncle, Beethoven's nephew Karl pointed the finger of blame at Schuppanzigh:

> I know though that the quartet was only not completely understandable because the first violin part went so badly . . . There were many disruptions. First nothing went together properly and then Schuppanzigh broke a string which contributed a lot, because he didn't have a second violin at hand.[13]

Schuppanzigh would have been playing on gut strings, much more prone to temperature fluctuations than modern synthetic alternatives. The mind boggles at anyone continuing to attempt this ferociously difficult music on a three-stringed violin in front of a paying audience. Where was his back-up set of Infeld Reds or Vision Titaniums?

The verdict that Schuppanzigh alone had been responsible for the inadequacies of the first performance was backed up by the actions of the other three players in the group. Shortly after that first concert violinist Karl Holz, violist Franz Weiss, and cellist Joseph Linke began to rehearse Opus 127 with Hungarian-born violinist Joseph Böhm, a violin professor at the Vienna Conservatory who would later teach such eminent violinists as Joseph Joachim and Jenö Hubay. In this formation the problematic new work was performed again on 23 March, this time with a radical change intended to aid both players and audience: the whole concert was devoted to Opus 127, which the musicians played twice separated only by a brief interval. Commenting on the experience of hearing both concerts a critic concluded that '[Beethoven] has provided a productive growth to his fame through the playing three times of this uncommonly difficult quartet.'[14]

Schuppanzigh continued to be blamed for the failure of Opus 127 at its first performance. When he asked to be given a second chance, he was passed over in favour of his ex-student, Joseph Mayseder (previously second violinist in Razumovsky's quartet). Under Mayseder two successful performances of the piece were given.

This music raised questions about the role of the first violinist: was a piece featuring such complex interweaving of melodies and accompaniments best served by the precise, authoritative playing of Mayseder or by Böhm's more expressive and less directorial approach? The new type of voice-leading that Beethoven described as a feature of his late quartets had resulted in greater independence for the other three voices. How could any rendition of Opus 127 be judged on the first violinist's performance alone? And yet, most of the discussion about Opus 127 in the conversation books revolved around the different characteristics of the first violinists. Karl Holz preferred Mayseder: 'He directs the other players while Böhm lets himself be directed.' Nephew Karl thought that with further study Schuppanzigh would play as well as the others, but judged Mayseder's performance the most brilliant and Böhm's the most expressive.[15]

Why hold the first violinist entirely responsible, I wondered as I opened the windows of my hotel room and rummaged in my suitcase for antacids. Humiliated by the failure of the first performance, Schuppanzigh had been forced to defend himself: 'I would have to lie [to say] that the passagework is too difficult for me, the ensemble is difficult.'[16] Whether or not he was lying about the individual difficulties, Schuppanzigh was not alone in pinpointing other challenges. Holz, perhaps distressed that Schuppanzigh had taken the brunt of the blame for the first performance, later admitted to Beethoven: 'If you had heard it, we would all four of us together have received a beating.'[17] Even Beethoven's brother Johann, one of Schuppanzigh's harshest critics, recognised the unusual nature of the part-writing: 'The interweavings are so tremendous that everyone could only manage to observe one instrument – because of this everyone wishes to hear the quartet four times.'[18] Fifteen months later Holz reported to Beethoven that one quartet even employed an extra person to beat time for the players.[19]

Attempting to banish the story of Schuppanzigh's failure and the accompanying repetitive melodic fragments of Opus 127 that whirled in my head, I lay in bed blasting singer/songwriter Jamie Cullum's recent CD *Twentysomething* through my headphones – an instant hit for Decca's new parent company, Universal. With commercial successes such as these, hopefully Decca would remain willing to release less profitable string quartet recordings – as long as they didn't have to pay for a conductor to beat time.

In the warm acoustics of St George's the next morning the first luxuriant *forte* E flat major chord provided a reassuring counterbalance to microphone nerves, a homogeneous quartet sound facilitated by the relatively narrow span of only two octaves between András' lowest note and my highest. This opening sequence of chords was marked *Maestoso* (majestic), Beethoven coaxing a symphonic richness of tone from the quartet by assigning double-stops to three of the four parts. What did I have to worry about? During a recording session we could repeat a passage as many times as we wanted. We planned to record the first movement in the morning session and would begin by playing the movement all the way through before retreating to the control room to assess our handiwork.

If only the slow opening section lasted longer than thirty seconds! Instead, a new *Allegro* demanded a complete transformation of sound and character. All the parts were marked *sempre p e dolce* (always quiet and sweetly), while above the first violinist's melody Beethoven added the instruction *teneramente* (tenderly). This sudden change so early in the piece was unprecedented in Beethoven's string quartets. Even the contrasting *pianissimo* theme at the beginning of Opus 59, no. 2 could be seen as coming out of the ferocious opening chords. But here, after only one bar of transition, an intimate melody ignored the majestic opening altogether: a public statement displaced by a private song.

Beethoven's nephew Karl reported that even Böhm and his quartet colleagues had faltered at the beginning of the more successful second concert and had to start the piece again. At least starting afresh in a recording session would be less embarrassing than in a performance. For me the challenge of the *teneramente* was how to control the change of bow technique from the sustained strokes near the bridge, necessary to play the *Maestoso* chords, to the faster bows over the fingerboard required for the tender melody. My aim was a transparent sound, but the extra adrenalin inspired by the presence of microphones and the gallon of tea I had downed at breakfast resulted in too fast a bow; any semblance of tenderness was scuppered by a shallow whistling sound as my bow skated over the surface of the strings.

We can't use that one. Just a first take: plenty of time to improve. Out of tune! Stop evaluating; just play. Karcsi and I not together. Microphones so inhibiting. What a wonderful opportunity to record this music. Saccharine! Concentrate! Relax bowing arm. Arpeggio unclear. JUST FOCUS ON THE MUSIC!

It was hard to banish this distracting counterpoint of unruly internal voices. No sooner had I achieved a more suitable bow speed than the character of the music changed yet again; after approximately ten seconds a *crescendo* led into a few bars of vigorous, rhythmic playing – a heroic character that left the *teneramente* far behind. After a brief pause András took over the same notes and rhythm that I had just played, but now with a quietly dancing mood. Four different characters in less than a minute!

Beethoven gave us no time to get settled with a mood or type of sound. A little further into the movement the opening *Maestoso* chords returned, breaking unexpectedly into a *pianissimo*, this time in the key of G major. The first chord now covered a three-octave span from the bottom cello G to the highest G in the first violin chord, creating a brighter sound. Again the *Maestoso* gave way to the same sweet *teneramente* melody that had dislodged the previous majestic statement, and we moved on to the development section.

Even though we had rehearsed and performed Opus 127 for several years, these changes continued to catch me by surprise. The microphones increased my discomfort, capturing mistakes I would shortly be required to hear again in the control room. I became fixated on the smallest flaws – a tiny bow scratch, a left-hand shift between two notes that was slightly blurry instead of a clean articulation.

We arrived at the most dramatic and emotionally unstable music of the movement, heralded by the fierce *fortissimo* tussle between the voices that we had recorded during our sound-check. Finally I could unleash some adrenalin, momentarily forgetting the microphones and playing with abandon. After so many quicksilver changes it was a relief to drum out insistent repetitions of the same note, interspersed with swooping arpeggios that covered the whole range of my violin:

The *Maestoso* chords tried once more to regain control of the music, now also marked *fortissimo*, with the extra strength of the quartet's sound underpinned by András' resounding open C and G strings played as a double-stop. The span between András' low C and my high C in the first chord was now four octaves, twice as wide as at the opening of the piece.

This *Maestoso* was only two-thirds as long as its previous iterations – there was even less time to inhabit the mood. As the first violin, viola and second violin in quick succession tried to re-establish the first lyrical melody, a fast, spiky accompaniment undermined the character. The music was suffering a crisis; none of the elements upon which the previous sections had been built was able to gain control. After a sudden *forte* chord we veered into the strangest section of the whole movement. Fragments of the opening melody were repeated obsessively, the three lower parts playing the same monotonous rhythm nineteen times in a row while I played another melodic fragment against them. After so much variety earlier in the movement the repetitions were particularly striking, an unwelcome thought lodging itself in the middle of the night, relentless and tormenting. After this unnerving section the return of the full *teneramente* melody provided relief.

The sudden changes of mood that dominated much of the movement made the last section stand out in contrast. The *Maestoso* was now banished for good, and the expansion of the melodic fragment into a tender reminiscence – the second passage we had tested at our initial sound-check – allowed us to enjoy the same mood for a full minute, roughly a sixth of the whole movement. This was the most magical ending to any first movement I could think of, unusual in the way it retreated to silence. It was not so much an ending as a question, an upbeat to whatever would come next.

After we had listened to our playing in the control room there was a pause, everyone reluctant to speak first.

'It's a subtle point but I think we could make an even more glowing sound in the *teneramente* – more perfumed, less direct,' said Roger.

'The end of the phrase could be more *grazioso*,' I added.

'The next *crescendo* gets too loud too soon,' said Karcsi.

As was frequently the case, hearing the first take

prompted a reassessment of priorities. The microphones threw a different light on our interpretation, raising new questions while making other concerns less significant. We sounded better than I had felt onstage, my technical slips not as glaring as I had feared.

Andrew scribbled notes in his score, listening and sometimes nodding his head. Our comments would give him a better idea of how to guide the session when we returned to the stage.

'What can we do with the opening *Maestoso* to make it more noble?' András asked.

'Is there a case for enjoying the middle of the notes more?' Andrew asked. 'I hear a lot of beginnings. Simon, could we listen to the opening again?'

We benefitted from Simon's quiet concentration as he followed our conversation, the opening material lined up and ready to play from his laptop before Andrew had finished talking. We agreed with Andrew that the opening chords were too aggressive, the beginnings of each note like a harsh consonant. The *fortissimo* outburst which I had enjoyed playing with such abandon sounded angry and chaotic: four dogs barking, snapping at each other's heels. We all sniggered at the effect, presumably not the reaction Beethoven was hoping for. Although the whole section was marked *fortissimo* we decided nonetheless to shape the dynamics: instead of playing each note of my arpeggios with equal intensity, I would grow towards the top, while the repeated individual notes would also start more quietly, increasing in volume towards the end of each group. Because Beethoven had given us fiercely independent lines, when I played more quietly the climax of another line could come through more clearly. Playing with abandon might feel liberating onstage but Beethoven's complex textures demanded careful organisation.

All of our comments so far pointed towards a common goal – how to bring out more dramatically the changes of character, dynamics and colour to make the music sound more immediate and spontaneous. Onstage I felt pushed and pulled by the extraordinary variety in the music, and yet in the control room our interpretation often sounded too predictable. Being shocked by the music myself would not create a vivid interpretation. By bringing into relief all the contrasts we hoped to convey more successfully the spirit of fantasy that Beethoven valued in his late quartets.

In the second half of the movement a question of balance arose. Above Karcsi I played an embroidered version of his melody.

'Karcsi has the tune. Ed, could you play less?' András asked.

'I can play more.'

'I don't know, Karcsi – then the whole level gets higher,' said András.

'But my descant is new and interesting,' I said. 'Do you want us all to play quieter all the time? Then we'll just sound careful.'

Exaggerating a colleague's unwelcome idea to make it seem less valid was a cheap trick. At times ill equipped temperamentally to deal with the demands of a recording session, I inflicted unfortunate flashes of impatience on my colleagues. Whereas on a concert day we could gear ourselves towards the evening performance, conserving energy and adrenalin earlier in the day, a recording session required us not only to repeat the same material over and over again with consistent emotional involvement, but also to re-evaluate our interpretation with determinedly sunny dispositions, cheerfully welcoming the suggestions of others. I was reminded of the laconic observation by another quartet player that the hardest aspect of quartet playing was the constant need to respect one's colleagues' opinions. At times I just wanted to forge ahead with my own idea, impatient with the complexities inherent in working so closely with three other musicians.

'Maybe it's time for another take,' Andrew suggested, sensitive to the dangers of prolonged discussion. The members of a famous string quartet had come to blows in the control room while making a recording for Decca many years previously. 'You can try that passage a few different ways. Later come on down and see which you prefer.'

We returned to the hall to concentrate on playing as well as we could. Our producer would not be a fifth person beating time, but his ears and ability to evaluate what we were doing released us from some responsibility. Andrew would gauge whether we were maintaining a high enough level of intonation and ensemble while helping us to achieve our musical goals.

After we had played the movement through several times we broke it down into smaller sections, allowing us to focus on the details we had discussed. It was gratifying to try shaping a phrase slightly differently on the spur of the moment and to hear Andrew's cheerful voice transmitted through a loudspeaker on the floor in front of us: 'That works; I've put a tick next to it.' Two hours into the session I was immersed in the satisfactions of recording, the possibility of pushing ourselves to improve an interpretation, of seeing the microphones not as a confining presence but rather as a catalyst for experimentation. My nocturnal worries about the role of the first violinist seemed less relevant: except for occasional questions of balance, the focus was on the group's interpretation and how to communicate the characters of the music more clearly for the microphones.

Towards the end of the session Andrew zeroed in on a few moments of bad ensemble and intonation that had eluded us so far, using tact and a few tricks to help us play to a higher level. 'The way that E floats through the air is a bit flat,' was a skilful way to avoid blaming a player: the note had doubtless been perfectly in tune when it left my violin, only to be tainted by impurities en route. Next Andrew asked us to rehearse one difficult passage that did not yet sound quite together. We dissected it, only two of us playing at one time, discovering that our bow-strokes were not quite unified. Then we reassembled the passage, playing one more version before asking Andrew if he thought it was ready to record. 'We left the mics on – it's good and we've already got it,' he said gleefully.

The technique of recording lots of material and then leaving our producer to stitch together the best version was open to the criticism that by using sophisticated technology to replace one sour note in a phrase with a note from a later version, we removed any sense of spontaneity from a recording. But having the freedom to select material from many different versions allowed Andrew to incorporate some of our more experimental or unusual bits of playing, just as a film director could splice together a scene from the many versions at his disposal. Towards the end of the session we played a freer, more exploratory version of the last section of the movement, safe in the knowledge that we had already played this section well enough. A recording allowed us to dig into music that we had already performed frequently, enriching our understanding of a piece over several days and gaining fresh ideas that we could, if we wished, apply to future concert performances.

Despite enjoying the latter stages of the session I was left with a heightened awareness of the many contradictions in the first movement of Opus 127. While the Opus 59 quartets featured an abundance of contrast and conflict that at times challenged comprehension, their forceful endings had the effect of tying up loose ends. In Opus 127 the experience of three *Maestoso* sections and the dramatic *fortissimo* outburst with its tortured aftermath could not be erased by a tender melody and a quiet ending. We had focused on bringing out details as vividly as possible, highlighting the very contrasts that had contributed to making Opus 127 hard to comprehend when it was first performed, but I was left with the thought that elements in this music would never be fully reconcilable.

The issue of comprehension dominated first reactions to Opus 127. When Böhm's quartet took the radical step of performing the piece twice in a row, it gave players and audience alike an additional opportunity to grasp its intricacies. The requirement to listen to the same piece in this way was an imposed medicine, reversing the contemporary custom whereby audiences could applaud insistently to request repetitions of a favourite movement. One could imagine some audience members applauding rather cautiously at the end of the second performance of Opus 127, for fear of encouraging yet further repeats. The first players might also have had mixed feelings about the double performance: although there were no other pieces in the programme to drain energy, nephew Karl reported that 'they were scarcely in a condition to play it two times . . . the heat was very great, they sweated a lot'.[20] But Karl observed to his uncle that the music was easier to understand this way.

In January 1826, Schuppanzigh was at last given another chance to perform Opus 127. Holz told Beethoven that although the rehearsals were still problematic, Schuppanzigh 'said that for the first time yesterday he really understood the *Adagio*, and that in his delight he would barely be able to play it'.[21] Unfortunately there are no reports on how this ecstasy of understanding influenced the subsequent performance. Schuppanzigh had doubtless benefitted from having more time to prepare the piece, but possibly Holz had exaggerated his account to reassure Beethoven that Schuppanzigh's second performance would be better than the first.

Considering the difficulties others experienced with Opus 127, Prince Galitzin's response from St Petersburg must have delighted Beethoven:

I have many thanks to give you, worthy Monsieur de Beethoven, for the precious parcel with the sublime Quartet that I have just received. I have already had it played several times, and I find in it all the genius of the master, and when the playing of it has become more perfect, the pleasure will be all the greater.

Galitzin instinctively recognised the advantages of repeated playing and listening, while attributing any imperfections to the performance rather than the composition. He urged Beethoven to print Opus 127 as soon as possible; 'such a beautiful masterpiece ought not to remain hidden for a single moment!'[22]

Two months later Galitzin again wrote to Beethoven, now posing a question that had arisen in rehearsal regarding whether one note in the viola part should be a D flat, or a C, one semitone lower. The fact that this note was not part of a prominent melody, but a demisemiquaver – over in an instant – shows how seriously the musicians in St Petersburg approached Beethoven's new quartet. Beethoven replied with a detailed explanation of why one of the musicians was correct in thinking the note should be a D flat, pleased that he had understood the composer's intent.[23]

Galitzin's positive reaction to Opus 127 was probably also influenced by the personal connection he had formed with Beethoven. Given the nature of correspondence between them during an almost three-year period while the prince awaited Opus 127, Beethoven's patron was predisposed to be enthusiastic about the music commissioned by and dedicated to him. On 3 August 1823, Galitzin had apologised to Beethoven for not having written sooner, distracted by the life-threatening illness of his only child. He went on to discuss financial arrangements for a manuscript edition of the *Missa solemnis* to which he had subscribed, before thanking Beethoven for having sent him two new pieces for piano: 'my wife who studies this instrument, and who is also one of your greatest admirers, is delighted with them, even beforehand.'[24]

Even beforehand. Just the thought of receiving Beethoven's latest piano music provided comfort for the prince and his wife. On 3 October 1823 Galitzin again confided in Beethoven that he and his wife, devastated by the loss of their child, had travelled to the southern provinces of

Russia in the hopes of improving her health. Galitzin remembered Beethoven's own problems: 'I hope that the infirmities from which you suffer will receive considerable relief by the treatments of the baths at Baden.'[25]

In his next letter Galitzin expressed his impatience to receive Opus 127, but also urged Beethoven to ignore such entreaties: 'One cannot command genius, rather must leave it alone.'[26] It was an instruction that Galitzin had some difficulty implementing:

16 June 1824: It is with very real impatience that I await the shipment of the quartet that you promised me.

28 July 1824: As for my Quartets my impatience requests them out of your friendship for me.

5 December 1824: I cannot express with what impatience I await the first of the Quartets.[27]

No wonder then that when the 'precious parcel' of Opus 127 finally arrived, the prince was so appreciative.

For Beethoven's contemporaries, experiencing one of his late quartets was like encountering a politically subversive newcomer who had just moved to town. Many would immediately discount his radical views; those prepared to give him a chance would struggle with contradictory impulses, not sure whether to admire or distrust his originality, baffled but intrigued by his erratic behaviour. However, as the newcomer became more familiar, to align oneself with those who claimed to understand him was to gain access to a special club.

After Böhm's double performance of Opus 127, a music

critic reported that 'the misty veil disappeared and the splendid work of art radiated its dazzling glory'.[28] In the presence of such illumination, how many audience members or players would have dared to admit that they were still stumbling around in the fog? While Schuppanzigh may have been sincerely delighted to feel he finally understood the *Adagio*, the proud violinist whose reputation had been sullied by the disastrous first performance was hardly likely to admit during rehearsals that he was still struggling.

Amongst Beethoven's friends and patrons, and chamber-music lovers more generally, the idea that further exposure to the late quartets would lead to greater rewards gained momentum. Prominent critics such as E. T. A. Hoffmann published analyses of Beethoven's music to aid comprehension, and in the summer of 1826 Bernhard Schott published Opus 127, enabling amateur string players to grapple with the music in the privacy of their homes. For pianists the publication of four-hand arrangements of several of the late quartets provided another means of engagement.

In a later age gramophone records would provide an ideal medium for enhancing understanding, enabling repeated performances, the comparison of different interpretations, and the opportunity to repeat a favourite movement as many times as one wanted without fearing for the fatigue of the performers or fellow audience members.

The wooden stage of St George's was golden in the early-evening light as we began to record the *Adagio* of Opus 127. We preferred to save slow movements for the evenings: tiredness from earlier sessions blunted the edges of adrenalin, making it easier to create the more meditative atmosphere often required by the music. After we had heard and commented on our initial take, we played the movement through twice in a row without talking in between, allowing ourselves to sink more deeply into the mood.

The opening violin melody begins with a simple scale, carried by a slowly lilting rhythm that opens out into increasingly wide, expressive intervals. At the end of the sixth bar András took the theme over from me, while I played a line meandering above the cello. This is a moment that has caused the cellist to stop – probably not only in our rehearsal studio – and ask the first violinist with varying degrees of patience who he thinks has the primary melody here. How did Schuppanzigh and Joseph Linke negotiate this passage? Having given up the right to present the first performance, would the cellist have expected Schuppanzigh to accompany him sympathetically or resigned himself to the inevitable ramifications of a first violinist's ego? At least Beethoven had given Linke the rights to what would be his next string quartet, Opus 132; and Linke would design a concert programme to show the cellist off to maximum advantage.

What a glorious descant! While András played a long note I reached up an interval of a minor seventh, an expressive vocal effect that conveyed a sense both of yearning and gratitude. As András' scale emerged, we played the same lilting rhythm as each other. To achieve a satisfactory balance (at least in my mind) I drew attention to the larger, more expressive intervals in my line but varied my sound so as to weave in and out of his melody. The intertwining of melodic material in this opening theme set the scene for an expansive movement consisting of six variations.

In the first variation of the *Adagio* roles and allegiances changed from beat to beat. All four parts played the same rhythm and dynamics as each other before the first violin emerged with an impassioned solo reaching more than two octaves higher than the second-violin part. Seconds later the cello played the most important line, an ascent into its highest register brought into relief by the descending notes of the three parts above it. Now the first violin melody was briefly the most prominent until the viola took it over halfway through the next bar. The variation ended with all four parts playing two notes in the same rhythm, separated by rests that provided air and clarity after such extended lyricism. Throughout the variation Beethoven reinvented the relationship between four lines that intermingled in such an intricate manner as to feel less like a clearly articulated conversation between individuals than an interchange of interior voices.

Stemming from the opening interchange between cello and violin, duets continued to be a feature throughout the movement. In the second variation, while the cello and viola provided a buoyant rhythm section, the two violins answered each other with fleeting runs, like lovers not yet entwined pursuing a humorous flirtation. In the fifth variation, during a whispered duet between viola and first violin, the music wavered in search of a new direction. Towards the end of the movement, while the first violin floated high above, the second violin and viola played hushed repeated notes that introduced an ominous tread, a rhythm that reminded me of the viola's pulse at the end of the slow movement of Schubert's 'Death and the Maiden'.

In all these examples the duets seemed more like private communications than dramatic conversations, a quality reinforced now in St George's by the absence of a specific audience. Although we were making a commercial recording for Decca, that evening in St George's it felt as if we were playing only for ourselves. In a way it seemed more appropriate that our interpretation would eventually be heard in living rooms, studies and cars – spaces more often private than public. While the Opus 18 quartets had been born in the environment of aristocratic salons, and the drama of the 'Razumovsky' quartets was suited to larger public spaces, the late quartets transcended such obvious boundaries. Perhaps this meditative, exploratory slow movement would be better appreciated in a setting far removed from stamping feet, sweaty brows, explosive coughs or any remaining trappings of concert etiquette.

After Virginia Woolf took her own life in 1941, her husband Leonard was so devastated that he did not have the energy to organise the music for her funeral. Leonard had previously agreed with his wife that the Cavatina from Beethoven's last Galitzin quartet, Opus 130, would be suitable music to have at one's cremation. When it came to the time, however, Leonard could not bring himself to suggest the Cavatina to the man making the funeral arrangements. Instead he listened to a recording of it alone in his home.

When I sat down to listen to our CD of Opus 127 almost a year after the recording session, the living room was graced by our enthusiastic border collie, who could see no other reason for me to sit on the floor than to play with her. As the opening chords rang out I braced myself like a patient in the dentist's chair. It was absurd to take such a defensive posture but I couldn't recall how we sounded: would the first transformation from majestic chords to intimate conversation or our solution to the ferocious and competitive *fortissimo* section be convincing? Listening to one of our CDs was rarely a relaxing experience: inadequacies grated while anything that sounded surprisingly good made me wonder if I could still perform to that level.

The first movement came across as more assured than it had felt during the session, the contrasts dramatic without sounding disjointed. Andrew had worked his magic in stitching together our best playing, while Simon's sound seemed to me a convincing mixture of clarity and warmth – even if I occasionally wondered if whoever was playing first violin came through clearly enough.

'Do you still like those strings?' Sam asked politely as a tail was waved in my face and a slimy rawhide bone dropped in my lap.

The reminiscence at the end of the movement had acquired poignancy since the recording session. Several weeks after we had finished recording all of the Beethoven quartets, Roger told us that he would be leaving the Takács and moving to Boston with his family. After ten years of touring he wanted the possibility of more dinners at home with his young daughters and his wife Natasha Brofsky, cellist in the Peabody Piano Trio, who had just won a teaching position at the New England Conservatory. When anyone leaves a quartet, however good the reasons, it is a wrenching experience for all concerned, challenging the person who leaves to replace or manage without the artistic satisfaction that comes from such a fulfilling way of life, while those who remain must go back to the drawing board and rebuild the quartet. Although we were on our way towards choosing three excellent finalists to play audition concerts with us in Boulder, our quartet life naturally felt suspended, even as we continued to play our last season of concerts with Roger.

While we had resolved questions about characters, balance and tempi in one particular way for the CD, no single recording could adequately explore the many interpretative possibilities the music suggested. This seemed particularly true for the ending of the whole piece, a section that Beethoven had himself modified between the first and second performances. According to the violinist Joseph Böhm, it had been Beethoven's experience of observing Böhm's quartet rehearse that encouraged him to change the tempo marking for the last section of the final movement. After a festive and at times rambunctious *Allegro*, the music winds down in dynamics and pace, the pulse briefly suspended as two violins trill on a long note. Out of this hiatus emerge fleeting *pianissimo* scales and the opening tune of the movement, whose transformed rhythm now adds buoyancy and lilt to the previously smooth legato line. The character of the ensuing climax and the last gestures of the piece depend largely on the choice of tempo.

Böhm later claimed he had suggested to his fellow musicians that they ignore Beethoven's instruction, *meno vivace* (less lively), 'which seemed to me to weaken the general effect . . . I advised that the original tempo be maintained, which was done, to the betterment of the effect.' The first violinist continued his modest narrative:

Beethoven, crouched in a corner, heard nothing, but watched with strained attention. After the last stroke of the bows he said, laconically, 'Let it remain so,' went to the desks and crossed out the *meno vivace* in the four parts.[29]

Apparently the often volatile master, far from being offended by the tempo alteration, was willing to change his mind at this late stage. Böhm admitted that the composer could not hear how the musicians were playing, but Beethoven had probably sensed the extra exhilaration and excitement that came with the change. As he watched the newly configured ensemble rehearsing his music, he glimpsed a different way of ending this complex piece – at least according to the testimony of a first violinist. In published editions Beethoven replaced the *meno vivace* with *Allegro comodo* (comfortably fast), a rather wishful indication in my experience, given the difficulties of the passage.

Recordings of Opus 127 take a variety of approaches to this last section. The Budapest Quartet play a fast tempo in their version recorded in Washington's Library of Congress in 1941, their last climax frenetic and exhilarating: a courageous choice considering that this was a live recording made with no editing sessions. They play the whole movement faster than many groups, as if Beethoven were determined to end this complex piece with a whirlwind of joyful activity.

Many groups, including the Takács, choose tempi that give the impression of *meno vivace* – the very instruction that Beethoven is purported to have deleted. One of the more dramatic examples of this comes in the Alban Berg Quartet's recording, where a markedly slower tempo results in a powerful and majestic climax that seems to refer the listener back to the *Maestoso* mood at the opening of the whole piece. If Beethoven had experienced this version he might have been inclined to reinstate his *meno vivace*, while the Budapest Quartet's rendition might have prompted him to add a *Presto* marking instead. The Takács ending was neither as fast as the Budapest nor as slow as the Alban Berg and I enjoyed our transparent, speculative sound at the beginning of the section. Beethoven created such an array of possibilities in Opus 127 that the piece can be concluded in a number of different ways.

As I listened back to Opus 127, holding my breath in anticipation of a particularly difficult passage, I was reminded of what a significant motivating force pressure had been during my time in the quartet, from the first year when I hoped to live up to the others' faith in me, through the period after Gábor Ormai's death when the 'Anglo-Magyar' foursome, as we became known, worked to re-establish a career. Even now I worried that just as Schuppanzigh's humiliation at the failure of his first performance had been exacerbated by positive reactions to the more successful performances of Böhm and Mayseder, perhaps our recording would be summarily dismissed in favour of other interpretations.

Being so immersed in the Opus 127 had been a polarising experience. Along with sleepless nights and long recording sessions came an increase in physical ailments. My newly found expertise on the differing attributes of over-the-counter wrist splints and anti-inflammatory gels was a subject of more concern but comparable interest at family dinners to ruminations on violin strings and soundpost adjustments. Along with such self-absorption had however come times of liberation, such as when we recorded the slow movement of Opus 127 – an evening when nothing else mattered except to be in the midst of the sublime interweaving of musical lines Beethoven had left for us. In my next decade of quartet life I hoped to find a way to strike a different balance: happiness in a quartet seemed to be more easily attained during those times when the particularities of personality receded and the music became the main story.

The challenge of evoking nostalgia in a musical phrase is easier for me than to succumb to it under other circumstances. To listen to a particular piece of music is to cede any control over what we remember and what we forget, a particular melody or chord change bringing with it overwhelming associations of a person, place or mood. While I was very grateful to have had the opportunity to record the Beethoven cycle with Karcsi, Roger and András, I would listen to the results only occasionally over the next decade. Our Beethoven discs came to represent both the work of four individuals trying their best on a given day in a specific time and place and also a tangible record of a fulfilling decade spent working together – a version to be proud of but by necessity also to evolve from, as we continued to explore other exciting musical possibilities with our new violist.

5

Convalescence: Opus 132

'Don't worry,' András told us backstage before a Sunday afternoon concert in June 2002 in Albuquerque, New Mexico. 'I'm taking blood thinners and there's a nitroglycerin pill in my tuxedo pocket: in the worst case just put it under my tongue.' His doctor had called the previous morning with the news that one of his arteries was blocked: András would need to have a stent inserted as soon as we returned to Colorado. Despite our qualms he insisted that there was no additional risk in playing the Sunday afternoon concert. Later that afternoon while performing Smetana's autobiographical quartet 'From My Life', the first movement of which expresses the composer's premonition of illness, we cast anxious glances at András any time the cello part was conveyed with excessive vigour. Following the procedure and a ten-day convalescence period, András was thankfully able to resume work in the quartet. Such a harrowing experience was another reminder of the underlying fragility of an enterprise that ties four people so closely to each other.

Several years after András' scare we acted on our lawyers' suggestion to buy life insurance policies for each other. Until we became accustomed to the arrangement illnesses were observed with particular attentiveness. At the end of a European tour I lay down in the check-in area of the Bordeaux airport, struggling with a flu virus as we pondered whether to cancel our next concert. Half an hour later we continued our journey and Karcsi squeezed my arm affectionately. 'For a while my Lamborghini was looking promising.'

Our mutual dependency is especially exposed when someone leaves a quartet. The basis of a string quartet is the work that four people do together over a long period of time, the empathy that we develop both personally and musically, and the bonds that are formed from shared experiences and challenges. When Geraldine Walther took the courageous step in 2005 to join the Takács as our violist, her enthusiasm and sense of adventure inspired a leap of faith, a choice to throw in her lot with three other musicians without knowing whether we would all stay in good health or how our musical and personal dynamics might evolve. Introduced to us by our North American manager, Seldy Cramer, Geri was an experienced chamber musician and soloist who had held the prestigious position of principal violist with the San Francisco Symphony Orchestra for twenty-nine years. During Geri's audition we were struck by the warmth and presence of her sound and how at home she seemed onstage, even during a performance of Opus 131 that had been put together on only three days of rehearsals. Plunging into quartet life, she admitted to sometimes waking up at 2 a.m. and practising for several hours to prepare the large number of string quartets we played during her first season.

'Who's going to have dinner with me tonight?' Geri's question at the end of our first rehearsal day on tour together was met by a shocked silence. Each quartet evolves its own system for balancing time together and apart. Although we travelled on the same planes we did not sit together: how could I enjoy catching up on episodes of *Friends* if next to me Karcsi was conscientiously studying the miniature score of a Bartók quartet? Staying in the same hotel was convenient only as long as our rooms were well enough separated to prevent someone's repeated G minor arpeggio ruining an afternoon siesta. On the few evenings that we kept free during a tour, Karcsi, András and I had become used to being independent. When the two Hungarians found themselves sitting in the same row as each other at a Leicester Square cinema it was an unfortunate coincidence to be laughed about years later, not a prelude to a hot date.

Orchestral tours had provided Geri with plenty of willing dinner companions; by contrast a Takács tour could feel bleak. With Geri's arrival we began to eat more meals together and to drive in a minivan instead of two cars. From the back seat she fed András (our designated driver) with biscuits, chocolates and bananas. Our rehearsing environment was similarly transformed by arrays of pastries and fruit, while birthdays were now celebrated in our studio with cakes and candles. But after a year of quartet experiences Geri's dinner question was subtly modified: 'If I don't get a better offer, can I have dinner with someone tonight?'

The arrival of a new player necessitates a re-evaluation of all aspects of our work together, from how we criticise and receive criticism of each other's playing to how much emphasis we place on the different elements that go into preparing a piece of music – including relative balance between the four voices, intonation, use of vibrato and conception of character. A new player negotiates the tricky balance between trying to fit in with a group's musical identity while wishing as soon as possible to be an equal participant, not a guest. Although Geri's arrival brought these issues to the fore, as had been the case when Roger and I joined the quartet, the factors necessary to sustain a string quartet still remain constant: we find ourselves varying the dosage of a familiar cocktail of medicines. To maintain the basics of good quartet playing we tune troublesome passages slowly, break down challenging rhythmic sections by playing in pairs, or sometimes check the consistency of our pulse with a metronome – all preventive care administered to keep potential ailments at bay.

After ten years of working together we find ourselves continuing to examine basic questions of character and pacing, a debate perhaps more easily inspired by a new player, but also essential amongst four players who may become too accustomed to working together. Some of our most useful yet contentious working experiences occur when we return to a piece of music after a time away from it, a re-examination that can provoke a crisis of sorts as we dismantle our interpretation in order to inject freshness into an approach that may have become too predictable. What new aspects of the music can be teased out by increasing blood flow to a phrase or reconstructing a transition whose joints have become tired? The hope is to reassemble an interpretation before a concert, but it doesn't always work that way. The most beautiful and rewarding pieces of music are also often the most elusive, the ideal prescription hardest to achieve.

Composed under unusual circumstances, the immense slow movement of Beethoven's Opus 132 is unlike any other music we play. In the winter of 1825 Beethoven's work on the second of the quartets for Prince Galitzin was hindered by a combination of abdominal ailments, the most dangerous of which threatened to turn into inflammation of the bowel – at that time usually a fatal condition. Dr

Anton Braunhofer, a respected professor at the University of Vienna, instructed Beethoven to give up wine, coffee and spices. The prescription was hardly innovative but perhaps because of the severity of both illness and doctor, the frequently obstreperous patient was briefly obedient. Braunhofer also urged Beethoven to travel to the town of Baden, sixteen miles south of Vienna. Beethoven had spent time at this spa town at least thirteen times between 1803 and 1824, drawn as much by the recuperative powers of the surrounding countryside as by the waters. When friends visited him in Baden, Beethoven liked to take them on his favourite walks through the nearby wooded valley of the Helenenthal.

As early as AD 70, Roman soldiers sought relief from their rheumatism in the sulphurous waters of Baden that erupted at temperatures between 24 and 37 degrees Celsius (75–98° F). Emperor Friedrich III highlighted another aspect of Baden's appeal in 1480 by bestowing a coat of arms upon the town that depicted a naked man and woman sitting in a small bathtub. Following the Reformation and Counter-Reformation controversy over mixed bathing was alleviated by the introduction of compulsory ankle-length bathing robes. Despite or perhaps because of these new restrictions, bathers often spent several hours in the water dining and drinking. From 1796 the presence of Emperor Franz II[1] and his court for two or three months during most summers ensured the prosperity of the spa town.[2]

Beethoven was not the first composer to be associated with Baden. Mozart's wife Constanze sought to improve her fragile health there and Mozart, although finding the town boring and not conducive to composing, visited her frequently. Haydn's estranged and bad-tempered wife

Anna Maria spent most of her last years in the spa town trying to alleviate her rheumatism. She made do with a portrait of her husband (which had the additional appeal of having been painted by her lover), who visited her there only in 1800 when she was dying.[3]

As Beethoven convalesced in Baden in May 1825 he jotted down in a conversation book the idea for the slow movement of Opus 132: a hymn giving thanks for his recovery and the reawakening of new strength. He entitled the completed slow movement *Heiliger Dankgesang eines Genesenen an die Gottheit, in der lydischen Tonart* (Holy Song of Thanks by a Convalescent to the Deity, in the Lydian Mode). It is in five sections: three based on a chorale, separated by two contrasting episodes, the first of which is entitled *Neue Kraft fühlend* (feeling new strength). Departing from the standard four-movement form of a string quartet, Beethoven placed this unique piece as the centrepiece of a five-movement work. More than fifteen minutes long, it is one of the most challenging movements in the string quartet repertoire.

In May 2014, at the Église Notre-Dame de la Gloriette in Caen, Normandy, not far from the site of the D-Day landings nearly fifty years before, we concluded our programme with Opus 132. Already backstage after the concert we began arguing about our interpretation, none of us happy with our performance. The next morning we sat around a small grey Formica table in our hotel, poking at scrambled eggs and continuing to debate how to play the prayerful chorale that sets the mood at the beginning of the *Heiliger Dankgesang*. The tempo marking is *Molto adagio* and we all play exactly the same slow rhythm.

'I don't feel a steady pulse,' Geri said. 'It's hard to think about the character if we don't know exactly where to play the next note.'

'If I lead too much then it gets restless,' I said, early morning not finding me at my most flexible.

'Maybe it would work better if we all led the pacing?' Geri suggested.

'Only if we can agree on the tempo,' said András. 'Otherwise we pull in different directions like last night. For me it's too restless. He's praying, not active.'

'Maybe you can pray in different tempi: there's not one right answer for that. I don't want it to sound restless either,' Geri said.

'We can make many things work but last night I didn't like the way we slowed down before each chorale phrase,' said Karcsi. 'Then it's hard to go on.'

The five phrases of the opening chorale are preceded by short contrapuntal preludes, each one exactly half the length of the chorale sections. One instrument enters, imitated after four notes by the next instrument, until everyone is playing. The first violin begins the first prelude, followed by second violin, viola and cello. The slowing down that Karcsi disliked occurred at the end of each of these imitative passages, like an organist grinding to a halt while the church choir waits impatiently to enter. At the beginning of each of the chorale phrases we aim to make a particularly delicate sound, but this is not sufficient reason to slow down: around the breakfast table we could at least agree that it made it more difficult to maintain a pulse.

In 1818 Beethoven had expressed the wish to compose a 'pious song in a symphony in the ancient modes'.[4] In his *Tagebuch* – the notebook Beethoven kept between 1812 and 1818 – he wrote that in order to write authentic church

music he would need in the first instance to study the eccle-
siastical chants of monks.[5] Beethoven was interested not
only in the older music of Palestrina, Bach and Handel, but
also in contemporary church practices: treatises in his personal library provided guidance on such subjects as how to
write a chorale or organ prelude. The *Heiliger Dankgesang*
was one outcome of an exploration that also bore fruit in
two vocal works composed just before Opus 132: the *Missa
solemnis* (Opus 123) and the choral finale of the Ninth Symphony (Opus 125), completed in 1823 and 1824 respectively.

Beethoven's use of the Lydian mode reduces harmonic
contrast and dissonance. The unusual length of each chord
and the decrease in tension imposed by the mode cause the
music to proceed so slowly that time comes close to standing still. In the earlier *Molto adagio* of Opus 59, no. 2, the
opening chorale-like bars create a comparable effect, but
after roughly forty-five seconds a new counter-rhythm in
the first violin part contributes a sense of forward direction.
Nineteen years later Beethoven dared to extend the opening chorale section of the *Heiliger Dankgesang* to almost
four minutes, with minimal rhythmic variety provided
only in the prelude sections that move in crotchets instead
of minims.

The Église Notre-Dame de la Gloriette should have
been an ideal setting for the *Heiliger Dankgesang*. A custom-
built stage raised us above a stone floor. On either side of
the church severe stone arches threw into relief an opulent
altar that faced us from the opposite end of the nave and
was surrounded by green marble pillars and gold orna-
mentation. This majestic space could have facilitated an
atmosphere of reverence, but during the concert I found it
hard to judge the pacing of this uneventful music, so con-

trasting to the frenetic tempo of our touring lives.

Forty-eight hours before our Caen concert we had been recording Shostakovich's Piano Quintet in Wales. After a long train journey I slept for twenty minutes, played a few speculative scales and arpeggios, and after a brief but frantic search located my hotel key card – efficiently lodged between my teeth – before walking to the concert venue. Struggling to maintain my energy onstage, I couldn't judge if we communicated an appropriate sense of repose or merely sounded lethargic.

After the concert I listened to several recordings of the *Heiliger Dankgesang*, curious to hear how different ensembles over the years had dealt with the issue of pacing. By far the slowest recording I could find was by the Busch Quartet, recorded in the 1930s. Despite the slow tempo there was never any sense of uncertainty about the way one chorale note moved to another: the end of one note was as quietly vibrant as the beginning of the next. In other recordings, faster and slower, there was a sense of the sound sagging as the players waited to play the next chord: perhaps our performance in Caen had suffered from this phenomenon. In addition my attitude to the role of the players in this unusual opening had caused difficulties. While any concert relies on the distinctive characteristics of an interpretation, I thought the opening of the *Heiliger Dankgesang* should come as close as possible to removing any sense of there being individual performers. Beethoven prays thankfully to a higher power and in so doing acknowledges his own insignificance: I wished our presence to be correspondingly self-effacing, the chord changes inevitable, as if not initiated by human action. In Caen this had caused me to be too withdrawn and unaware of the musical impulses around me.

Nonetheless the audience had responded enthusiastically to our performance. Although we needed to iron out differences in our approach to the chorale, perhaps the causes of our dissatisfaction were not entirely musical. My discontent stemmed in part from a petty rebellion against our situation. As sometimes happens towards the end of a demanding tour, I felt burdened by how closely bound socially and musically we were to one another. I had been more easily able to dig into the dissonant individual lines of the Shostakovich quartet in the first half of the concert than to negotiate the deceptively simple consonance of Beethoven's chorale.

In other circumstances we found better ways to acknowledge this aspect of quartet life. During the last half-hour of our Boulder rehearsals András would sometimes remind us that he was teaching a lesson immediately afterwards.

'Then we had better rehearse right up until 6 p.m.,' I said.

'We don't want you to be lonely: you'll miss us,' Geri said.

'You read my thoughts exactly.'

'Don't worry, András,' said Karcsi. 'I can come back afterwards for an extra rehearsal – just the two of us.'

'How nice it is to have dear colleagues who understand me – let's stop eight minutes early. I'm sure everyone will pack up quickly.'

A humorous recognition of our harried mental states towards the end of a long tour might have aided our Caen performance. Over the next few months we would seek to capture the grateful, serene mood of the opening chorale in a variety of settings: during concerts at the Aspen and Edinburgh festivals later that summer, but more pressingly in the Théâtre de la Ville in Paris in two days' time. In its dry acoustics I doubted that we would be able to sustain the extremely slow tempo of the Busch Quartet, but by focusing more on the overall melodic line instead of just the mechanism of each note change, we could achieve a more unified effect. At the stage rehearsal in Paris I planned to try a less self-effacing approach. Instead of sitting back in my chair with my eyes occasionally shut, I would assume a more forward posture, playing into the group and trying to sense how my colleagues felt the pulse so that I could sign the changes with greater clarity. To be so attuned to three other people's physical and mental condition could at times feel confining, and yet the right sort of preparation enabled us to move as one onstage. Hopefully we would be able to combine Geri's desire for a clear pulse, Karcsi's wish not to slow down before the chorales and András' need for a more peaceful prayer.

Throughout his life Beethoven turned to nature for spiritual and physical rejuvenation. In 1808 he had celebrated the countryside in his 'Pastoral' Symphony, nature providing a model for crisis and recovery that was mirrored in the music: the last movement was a 'Shepherd's Song' which expressed gratitude after a storm. More than once, Baden was the setting for serious illness and convalescence. Writing from the spa resort in the summer of 1813, Beethoven asked his friend, patron and piano student, Archduke Rudolph, the half-brother of Franz II, to excuse any lapses of behaviour as being the result of mental confusion, explaining that 'the glorious beauties of Nature and the lovely surroundings of Baden will restore my balance'.[6] Yet despite Beethoven's creation of a pastoral idyll, his verdict in 1822 on a regimen of thirty baths prescribed by his doctor to cure yet another illness was lukewarm: 'I cannot declare with certainty that there has been a definite improvement. All the same I fancy that thanks to the good effects of the baths the trouble will be arrested, not completely cured.'[7]

During May and June 1825, as Beethoven shaped the *Heiliger Dankgesang* into a piece of five sections alternating between the Hymn of Thanks and New Strength, his reports on his health to his doctor and nephew were not always consistent with the narrative of recovery embraced in the music. Admittedly a letter from Beethoven to Dr Braunhofer on 13 May included a grateful gift in the form of a musical canon, set to the words, 'Doctor, close the door 'gainst death, notes shall inspire my breath.' However, written in the form of a fictional dialogue between doctor and patient, the letter was not exactly a resounding endorsement of professional efficacy. Beethoven suggests to his doctor that he may need more powerful medicine. In the imaginary reply Braunhofer recommends that his patient alternate the methods of two well-known contemporary doctors, Brown and Stoll, who practised entirely contradictory methods. Beethoven's expression of gratitude is additionally undermined by the admission that he took only one dose of the previous medicine prescribed by Braunhofer before losing it.[8]

On 17 May Beethoven reported to his nephew Karl that he was beginning to compose again. But the next day, complaining of diarrhoea, he considered ignoring the doctor's embargo on coffee because Braunhofer's prescriptions were sometimes ineffective. 'And on the whole he strikes me as very narrow-minded and, therefore, a bit of a fool.'[9] Beethoven once again attempted to visit the doctor in Vienna on 4 June but did not find him at home. The composer was in a lugubrious mood on 9 June, complaining to his nephew of both the cold weather in Baden and being constantly alone: 'In any case the grim reaper will not grant me much more time.'[10]

Although his initial idea for the *Heiliger Dankgesang* was inspired by his most recent brush with death and subsequent convalescence, Beethoven's prayer of thanks was a statement of faith, an expression of gratitude untouched by the fluctuating state of his health and moods.

'We sorted this out at breakfast yesterday: do we need to rehearse it?' Onstage at the Théâtre de la Ville I tried to cover my anxiety with a joke and was grateful that the others laughed. We all wanted to have a better experience than in Caen performing the *Heiliger Dankgesang*, even if we were not exactly sure how to achieve it.

I was happy to be back in the Théâtre, a venue at which we play almost every season, invited by the Hungarian director of music, Georges Gara, who always lightens the mood of our stage rehearsal by teasing his compatriots. Renowned for its avant-garde theatre and dance productions performed beneath nine hundred seats that rake steeply upwards from the stage, the theatre provides a far less reverential atmosphere than the Église Notre-Dame in Caen. Indeed the only time we ever encountered a heckler was here, during a joint programme with the Hungarian group, Muzsikás, which explored Béla Bartók's interest in folk music. We performed Bartók's Fourth String Quartet, but in between movements the players from Muzsikás jumped up from their seats and improvised excerpts on traditional folk instruments. Although this placed Bartók's unique sound world in the context of the folk music that informed his musical language, during the first Muzsikás demonstration in the Théâtre de la Ville an audience member shouted repeatedly, 'Que le quatuor joue!' (Let the quartet play!) Other audience members hushed him, but when a violinist from Muzsikás again stood up, the heckler continued to register his outrage, this time countered by equally loud exclamations from other members of the audience eager to shout him down – an admittedly tamer descendant of the riot that accompanied the first performance of Stravinsky's *Rite of Spring* in Paris in 1913.

The first performances of Opus 132 suffered from no such disturbances. Scarred by the initial negative reactions to Opus 127, Beethoven and his quartet musicians adopted a cautious approach, introducing Opus 132 at first for an invited audience in private concerts on 9 and 11 September 1825 before presenting the first public performance in November. The English musician Sir George Smart attended the first concert, held in the hotel rooms occupied by the Berlin-based publisher Maurice Schlesinger (who would later publish both Opus 132 and Beethoven's last complete quartet, Opus 135). Smart reported that the piece was played twice, an imitation of the successful device employed by Böhm and his colleagues at the second performance of Opus 127. Beethoven conducted from the score and himself provided the only disruption to the concert when he seized the second violinist Karl Holz's instrument to correct a bow-stroke he saw was incorrect: unable to hear the pitches, he played it a quarter-tone too flat.[11]

As we gingerly started to rehearse the *Heiliger Dank-gesang* onstage in Paris, potential audience reactions were of minor concern to me. How would Karcsi, Geri and András like our interpretation today? We played the whole of the opening section without talking before I stopped to canvass opinions. 'Good.' 'I like it now.' 'Better.' No one was eager to disturb a perhaps fragile equilibrium, more inclined just to let the quartet play. Even after twenty years of working in the quartet I was surprised by this sudden progression from disagreement to consensus – perhaps we should eat breakfast together more frequently. Between our conversation and the rehearsal thirty-six hours later, an unspoken accommodation had been reached. There were no miraculous revelations or dramatic changes of interpre-tation, but the mix of dissonant musical opinions rubbing against each other onstage in Caen was enough to encour-age a modification of positions. I signed the changes of note more clearly, resigned to the reality that a performer cannot be entirely self-effacing; Geri enjoyed the steadier pulse; András played more sustained notes in the bass; and Karcsi suggested that we risk playing more quietly. 'But who I am?' he asked. 'Who I am?' we repeated, enjoying the sen-timent and its expression – a happy progression from our prickly individualism of the previous day.

By the simple means of a C sharp in the second-violin part and a short *crescendo*, Beethoven takes us out of the Lydian mode and the *Heiliger Dankgesang* into the bracing key of D major for the new section entitled *Neue Kraft fühlend*. The easy displacement of one section by another is a significant and challenging feature throughout this move-ment. By giving the contrasting section a title Beethoven provides a seemingly unambiguous guide to the character of the music, but the sudden shift of mood after four minutes of serene chorale is not easy to achieve.

We set off at a slightly faster tempo than usual. While Geri and András provided buoyant rhythm, I scurried up my ascending scales, enjoying the sparkling interplay between the two violins. After only a few bars András stopped.

'Isn't it too fast? Sounds like Popeye.' Karcsi and András reminded us of the cartoons they had seen as teenagers on television in Budapest: Popeye the hapless sailor, butt of everyone's jokes, who acquires superhuman strength by eating spinach. 'I'm Popeye the Sailor Man, I'm strong to the finish 'cause I eats me spinach, I'm Popeye the Sailor Man . . .'

Geri liked the energy of our latest version, and András conceded that perhaps we just needed to become settled with a new idea that I had overstated at first for fear of encountering opposition. In many recordings, including our Decca version, I find the opening gestures of new strength too weighty and earthbound, as if the convalescent had jumped out of bed, raised a loaded barbell and let forth an elated cheer of rediscovered testosterone. Given that Beethoven's recoveries were often short-lived, I wanted to try a lighter approach to the *Neue Kraft*: a spring bud vulnerable to late winter frosts. Popeye was not the ideal result: the music should sound fresh, not manically frivolous and bursting for a fight.

Judging the energy level of the musical characters we communicate onstage can be difficult: what for one person is an invigorating sense of drive seems gratingly pushy to another. The violinist Sylvia Rosenberg once described to me the process of assimilating musical ideas as the 'Three

Bears Syndrome': extremes tried out before the ideally warmed porridge, sized chair or sprung mattress can be achieved. As we played the *Heiliger Dankgesang* in the Théâtre de la Ville later that day, below an attentive if at times bronchial audience of nine hundred, I relished the unity of purpose demanded and for the time being realised in our opening chorale. Although in the *Neue Kraft* section the first violinist perhaps continued to sound overly forti-fied by spinach, that afternoon we were a happier quartet, successful cooperation appreciated all the more for having eluded us in Caen.

In July 2014 we reached the end of the first *Neue Kraft fühlend* in Harris Hall, built underground in the meadow-land above the Roaring Fork River, a mile north-west of downtown Aspen. Behind us onstage sat sixty students, many wearing T-shirts and shorts, their skin betraying varying degrees of exposure to the Colorado sunshine. Since 1998 we have performed concerts at the Aspen Music Festival as part of an annual two-week residency during which time we also coach student string quartets.

Twenty-four years ago I was myself a student in Aspen and loved to practise late into the evening in one of the small wooden cabins that stood adjacent to a bubbling stream, inhaling the scent of pine needles that pervaded my room as the temperature cooled. The setting encouraged a spirit of exploration amongst students and visiting artists alike. When the conductor James DePreist rehearsed Beet-hoven's 'Pastoral' Symphony that summer he allowed us into his working process, asking for the same passage to be played twice but with two different phrase shapes, admit-ting that he wasn't yet sure which one he would choose

– we would have to be on our toes in the concert. Nature provided its own unruly counterpoint during the performance in the Aspen Tent: as we reached the 'Shepherd's Song' of thanks following the storm, thunder rumbled inconsiderately down the valley.

Like Baden in the nineteenth century, Aspen has become a luxurious haven, a ski resort that also offers a variety of activities during the summer, including classical and jazz concerts and an Ideas Festival. Returning there each year brings with it the possibility of recuperation amongst mountain scenery that has been enticing travellers for over a century.

With the dwindling of the gold rush came a new interest in Colorado as a place of rejuvenation. From 1890 Colorado Springs became a leading convalescent centre for tuberculosis patients drawn to the almost year-round sunshine and dry air. Forty miles down the valley from Aspen, Glenwood Springs opened its Hot Springs Pool in 1888. Aspen was slower to attract tourism following its silver bust, reinventing itself as a ski town only in the 1940s. Chicago industrialist Walter Paepcke and his wife Elizabeth founded the Aspen Institute in 1949, envisioning a place where political leaders, intellectuals, artists and musicians could gather to exchange ideas and find new inspiration.

In addition to boasting the Rocky Mountain National Park, Mesa Verde, the Great Sand Dunes and a plethora of spiritual retreats, Colorado has recently legalised marijuana, facilitating yet one more form of medicinal and recreational relief. The Colorado Symphony, based in Denver, took advantage of this development to introduce a private concert series, *Classically Cannabis: the High Note Series*, encouraging patrons to bring their own marijuana to enhance their musical experience. A Hot Tub Beethoven Quartet Cycle – perhaps performed for patrons in ankle-length robes – is surely just around the corner.

As we embarked on the second *Molto adagio* I tried to banish from my mind the list of eminent and discerning performers and teachers who were listening in Harris Hall that evening, remembering James DePreist's inspiring precedent of exploring musical alternatives in the presence of inquisitive students. When I was one of those eager participants many years ago I envied the aura of success surrounding the guest artists. Now I felt the contrast between my privileged state as an established musician, expected always to perform to a high level, responsible for and dependent upon the well-being of my quartet colleagues, and those unencumbered student days when I practised late at night by a mountain stream.

In the second *Molto adagio* Beethoven loosens the bonds of the chorale. Already the first introductory prelude is liberated from the repeated crotchets by the addition of quavers and dotted rhythms that gently propel the music forward. The basic structure of prelude and chorale phrases remains unchanged, but while the first violin plays the original melodic line of the chorale – an octave higher than previously – the other parts enjoy greater rhythmic and melodic freedom, traversing wider intervals that transform the opening section's serene prayer. With frequent octave leaps the cello seems especially unfettered – seeking and searching as it quietly probes the smooth lines of the chorale melody. If the opening chorale was a serene valley path, now the path has reached higher ground: the walkers look upwards, imagining what lies beyond. The increase in rhythmic momentum can encourage us to play faster and faster. I resisted the impulse, knowing that András would affix me with a beady eye if I pushed ahead too enthusiastically.

We reached the end of the second *Molto adagio* section in Harris Hall and the mood was again displaced by a *Neue Kraft* section, this time merely entitled *Andante* – since this is the second time we hear this music, the strength is no longer newly found. The brevity of these short transitions has a cumulative effect. Serene prayer / feeling new strength / prayerful again / return of strength: the sudden changes make the character of each section seem increasingly provisional, the rhetoric of recovery and new strength open to question.

Perhaps a song of thanks will always be vulnerable to incongruity. In February 2010 Karcsi struggled through the *Heiliger Dankgesang*, manipulating his violin through unnatural angles to accommodate the restricted motion of his bowing arm. Opus 132 was the last piece we performed with him before he underwent shoulder surgery, his rotator cuff badly enough torn that I wondered whether he would ever be able to play the violin again. We played the *Heiliger Dankgesang* while wishing fervently for a successful operation, the music an expression of faith that countered our situation. Frequently at odds with his doctors, Beethoven would have appreciated Karcsi's humorous jibe to his surgeon: 'If you screw this up you'll be playing the violin for the rest of your life.' Several months later Karcsi returned with a good as new rotator cuff that now enables by far the fastest tremolo bowing in the quartet.

Fragility was in the air that summer in Aspen. While I revisited my favourite hikes and practised in the cabins at the music school, at times reawakening the spirit of my student days, no tuberculosis patient would have benefitted from an atmosphere tainted with ash and smoke from the forest fires that raged throughout the west. On every slope was evidence of the destruction of pine trees by mountain pine beetles that had survived the recent mild winters. For how many years would Aspen be a haven if we continued to destroy our environment? In this context I found the anguished outbursts in the outer movements of Opus 132 easier to perform than a slow movement that required such sustained serenity.

Perhaps it is precisely under unlikely circumstances that the *Heiliger Dankgesang* can have its greatest effect, striving for an emotional state all the more valuable for being hard to attain. For Beethoven the *Heiliger Dankgesang* represented an escape from his own situation as much as a celebration of his recovery. As Beethoven worked on Opus 132 in May and June 1825, Karl bore the brunt of his uncle's loneliness, suffocating affection and expectations. Following the death of his brother Kaspar Anton Karl in 1815, Beethoven had begun a protracted conflict with Karl's mother Johanna to gain the guardianship of his nine-year-old nephew. From 1820 Beethoven assumed co-guardianship, at first with Karl Peters, a friend and tutor, and from 1825 with Dr Reisser, Deputy Director at the Polytechnic Institute where Karl studied. But this was not a carefree time for the young student. Beethoven remained possessive and suspicious, deeply resentful of any time that Karl tried to spend with his mother. Beethoven thought of himself as Karl's father, addressing the youth as his son in many of the letters he wrote to him. Viewing the relationship with his surrogate son as a final chance in life to establish a close familial bond, he sought to influence Karl's studies, social behaviour and financial habits, urging his nephew to balance conscientious studying with his obligations to his uncle.[12]

Karl could never be certain whether he was dealing with a needy uncle or the severe guardian who could write from Baden at the end of May 1825: 'God is my witness that my sole dream is to get away completely from you and from that wretched brother and that horrible family who have been thrust upon me.'[13] In August the following year, the twenty-year-old Karl would make his own effort to escape the suffocating and burdensome relationship with his uncle, ascending to the ruins of Castle Rauhenstein where he attempted to shoot himself twice in the head as he overlooked the Helenenthal, the scene of some of Beethoven's happiest pastoral explorations. The botched effort was more likely a cry for help than a firm intention to kill himself.

Karl's desperate attempt was in large part a reaction to the perfectionism and neediness that plagued Beethoven's interactions with his friends, relatives, patrons, publishers, copyists and housekeepers. Craving ideal relationships like the notes of a harmonious chorale, each dependent on and enhancing the others, Beethoven provoked one dissonance after another in his relations with Karl, finding refuge only in his music: 'If I had nothing higher to enjoy, I should find my life quite unbearable.'[14]

For the 2014 Edinburgh Festival, commemorating the hundredth anniversary of the outbreak of World War I, director Jonathan Mills encouraged artists to programme works that were written as a response to suffering. In our two August concerts we featured Janáček's two string quartets, Smetana's 'From My Life' and Barber's *Adagio*.

We finished the concerts with Beethoven's Opus 59, no. 2 and Opus 132.

During the early stage rehearsal before our second morning concert at the Queen's Hall, we found ourselves discussing the lighter music that precedes the *Heiliger Dankgesang*. In the middle section of the previous movement Beethoven borrows from his earlier *Musette* and *Allemande*, both pieces originally composed for piano, and crafts them into a dance medley. The simple harmonies and cheerful character give the music a childlike veneer, but Beethoven subjects the naive surface to a displaced and shifting metre: often the last beat of the bar sounds like the first, and in case the dancers think they can still dance easily in three, the occasional insertion of duple time throws them into confusion. Nothing is ever quite as it seems.

András worried that again we were playing too fast – Popeye lurking in the wings. Geri reminded us that we shouldn't overthink this lighter music: a carefree, easy-going attitude would create much-needed contrast with the slow movement. I enjoyed the suggestion of irreverence but felt the opening of this Trio as a dream. My part begins with a bagpipe imitation of sorts, the ascending notes of an A major arpeggio and melody underpinned by an open string drone, while Karcsi yodels beneath. But Beethoven marks the first violin *dolce* (sweetly); I like to play it as a memory, not with the thrilling and pungent reediness of the real bagpipes we heard on the street the previous night.

Towards the end of the section there is no doubting the rustic character of the viola and cello's loud and rude interruption of the dance: they are a couple of belligerent intruders shattering the idyllic atmosphere before making an equally abrupt exit. The bagpipes return, but for the first time the *piano dolce* evolves into a long *crescendo* that lasts a full ten bars. By omitting a top dynamic at the end of the *crescendo* Beethoven raises a question. A ten-bar *crescendo* beginning from *piano* could grow very loud indeed, but is the composer's omission significant? Do the bagpipe players joyfully take centre stage or is their last entrance more suggestive, distant music floating in on a change of wind? I prefer an interpretation that can leave open the possibility of both in the same way that Beethoven shifts metre throughout the section, refusing to supply the dancers with a reliable downbeat – the end of the Trio now blurring the line between reality and memory.

Carefree or nostalgic; sacred or profane; rude or idyllic; real or dreamlike? We continued to explore the contradictions in the music, performing laser surgery on our Trio as we tweaked details of character, phrasing, and dynamics, trusting that our patient would recover in time for the concert.

Towards the end of Aldous Huxley's novel *Point Counter Point*, published in 1928 a year after the centenary of Beethoven's death, Maurice Spandrell rushes out to buy a gramophone player so that he may listen to the recently released recording of Opus 132 by a Hungarian string quartet (part of the first complete Beethoven quartet cycle recorded by the Léner Quartet for Columbia Records). Spandrell invites Mark Rampion and his wife Mary to come to his house, hoping to persuade Rampion, an atheist, of the power of the *Heiliger Dankgesang*. 'You can't understand anything until you have heard it . . . it proves all kinds of things – God, the soul, goodness – inescapably.'[15] The scene has a melodramatic backdrop. Spandrell, a murderer, has planned his own death – an armed confrontation with the police which will occur at his London flat while the last section of the *Heiliger Dankgesang* plays in the background.

For Spandrell the hymn sections represent something more than the gratitude of a convalescent:

> It was the serenity of the convalescent who wakes from fever and finds himself born again into a realm of beauty. But the fever was 'the fever of the living' and the rebirth was not into this world; the beauty was unearthly, the convalescent serenity was the peace of God. The interweaving of Lydian melodies was heaven.[16]

While Spandrell changes the side of the record and winds up his new record player, Rampion resists the music, hearing in it weakness, merely the vision of someone whose body has let him down: 'Why can't he be content with reality, your stupid old Beethoven?' As they listen to the last section Rampion is almost convinced by the power of the music, but to give in to it would be a denial of life. Rampion looks across at Spandrell, whose eyes are closed: 'His face was grave and serene, as though it had been smoothed by sleep or death.'[17] The police knock at the door and Spandrell rises from his seat to meet his fate.

While picturing the bloody scene of Spandrell's death does nothing to increase my enjoyment of the *Heiliger Dankgesang*, the argument between Spandrell and Rampion elucidates the vying elements in the music. For Spandrell the music expresses a release of the soul rather than merely thankfulness for the body's recovery. Rampion resists the interpretation: if he had been allowed to meddle with Beethoven's manuscript, the movement would have

finished with another section of *Neue Kraft*, the body tri-
umphantly resisting the release of the soul. Repeated illnesses forced Beethoven to confront his mortality. The
Heiliger Dankgesang begins by celebrating recovery but
eventually breaks away from this cycle, seeming in its latter
stages to embrace a liminal state. Beyond the obvious religious associations of the chorale, what lends the music this
transcendent quality, prompting an atheist recently to
admit backstage that, whenever he hears the *Heiliger Dankgesang* he briefly believes in God?

In the final slow section Beethoven continues the transformation of both the chorale theme and the prelude music.
The latter, already liberated by the introduction of more
varied rhythms in the second *Molto adagio*, is now further
changed. The original

became in the second *Molto adagio*

and now becomes

The changed rhythm introduces a lilt and bend to the same
notes, making the theme more personal; it is an organist no
longer constrained by the conventions of contemporary

church practice, improvising in his own way. Beethoven writes above this transformed theme, *Mit innigster Empfindung* ('with the innermost sentiment', or 'with the most private feeling'). No longer merely a prelude to the chorale, this private confession draws our ears to it like the soliloquy of an understudy who has now assumed a more important role.

In the meantime the four homogeneous strands that made up the opening chorale have been teased apart, and the initial melody of eight notes shortened to five. The chorale is treated now as a fugue in four parts, one played after another – a dissolution of the homogeneous choir. The most miraculous element of these transformations is that Beethoven achieves them simultaneously. Whereas previously the prelude and chorale had alternated, now they are commingled, one providing counterpoint for the other, the lines between different elements blurred.

Towards the end of the movement the number of notes in the chorale is further reduced from five to three and then to two – an F and E one semitone apart that move up through the quartet, starting in the cello and ending four octaves higher in the first violin, evaporating as the music fades to silence.

In his *Tagebuch* Beethoven had copied down extracts from *Die Schuld*, a play by the German dramatist Amandus Gottfried Adolf Müllner which Beethoven contemplated setting to music. One of the extracts Beethoven selected associates the fading away of a piece of music with death. Elvira sits alone with her harp playing ever more quietly, her last note like a drop on a pond whose rings gradually disperse 'in the distance on the pond's flowery banks':

So would I, one day, like to soar on high
And fade away into the better life.[18]

After the intermingling of chorale and prelude and the dis-solution of the chorale, the *Heiliger Dankgesang* itself dis-solves into silence, the last Lydian chord left up in the air as the soul takes flight.

Many quartet enthusiasts describe the *Heiliger Dank-gesang* as their favourite movement from the whole Beet-hoven cycle, citing its transcendent qualities. Paul Nelson, director of the concert series at Middlebury College in Ver-mont for thirty years, who booked the Takács for our first Beethoven cycle after I joined the quartet, articulated a variation on this theme. The opening chorale is his favour-ite moment in the Beethoven quartets because it reminds him of the lugubrious Swedish hymns he sang every Sun-day, growing up in northern Iowa. The music not only reconnects him to his past but allows him to invent it anew: sombre hymns were perhaps not always appreciated by a six-year-old boy but can be revisited now through the lens of Beethoven's chorale.

For the Takács, too, this movement has provided some of our most memorable experiences. In Edinburgh at the Queen's Hall that morning, in my mind at least, occurred the magical communication between audience and per-formers that the greatest music enables. Of all the many ways we experience an audience – hearing a heckler, seeing the enthusiastic smiles of students onstage – the most satis-fying interaction is the silence of an audience under certain conditions during a concert. From the first note of our per-formance of the *Heiliger Dankgesang* at the Queen's Hall, the level of silence was so total as to make it an indispensable part of the music. The unique qualities of the venue played their part: a decommissioned church converted into a rehearsal and concert space retained the memory of worship without the associations of a particular religion. In addition to the audience below us a horseshoe-shaped balcony placed listeners around and above us, some of whom stood for the entire concert, craning over the heads of others to see the performers.

The degree of stillness in the hall during the last section of the slow movement encouraged us to linger over some of our favourite moments, stretching out the chords in the ecstatic climax that preceded the ethereal ending, waiting longer than usual after an elemental *pianissimo* chord that uses only the uncompromisingly bare intervals between an A and D and seems to look back even further than the Lydian mode. We were taken far out of ourselves, liberated from the confines of individual personalities as we surrendered to the music, a blissful state made possible all those years ago by a lonely convalescent not entirely confident of his recovery. Above all, this is why we play string quartets, weathering the sometimes fragile nature of our dependent relationships to enjoy such concert experiences that reaffirm the leap of faith we have made in each other.

It's a shame that the police didn't knock on Spandrell's door a little later. The sceptic Rampion would have appreciated the sharp dose of reality Beethoven delivers immediately after the slow movement. Inserted rather late into the score, the *Alla marcia, assai vivace* replaced what would have been a gentler let-down, a genial dance which Beethoven would instead use as the fourth movement of his next quartet, Opus 130. The rigid dotted rhythms of the march create a jarring contrast with the previous music. And again all is not as it seems. Unlike the *Thème russe* which strides confidently into Opus 59, no. 2, this march would perplex an unsuspecting regiment marching off to war. It's not clear what is a downbeat or an upbeat, and a pause after only a few notes increases the confusion. This is a far cry from *Wellington's Victory*, which Beethoven had composed for the Congress of Vienna a decade earlier. The composer had reason now to take a different view of the military. In the summer of 1824 he had been horrified by Karl's desire to join the army and would resign himself to his nephew's military ambitions only after Karl's attempted suicide two years later.

Should the *Alla marcia* have a sarcastic edge or should we play it only with good humour? Both versions could be convincing: in any case the music is shockingly mundane and, for the performers at least, a refreshingly cold shower after the demands of the previous movement. It is my favourite juxtaposition in all the Beethoven quartets, daring and irreverent – the invention of someone not ready to give up the ghost quite yet.

Alternative Endings: Opus 130

Sometimes I wish he had not composed the fugue. Its themes threaten and chase me, the opening subject stark and uncompromising:

and the counter-subject with its leaping intervals and relentless dotted rhythms:

Fragments of the two compete in my head, spawning restlessness, scorning contentment.

Throughout the opening pages of the *Grosse Fuge* the voices cry out against their interdependence – as close as a Beethoven string quartet gets to conveying a chaos of emotional extremes easier to evade than confront. No wonder that a reviewer of the first performance of Opus 130, while conceding that with increased familiarity the most difficult passages might become easier to understand, raised the possibility that Beethoven's inability to hear his own music had led to some of his more bizarre writing. His first impression of the almost fifteen-minute-long *Grosse Fuge* was damning: 'incomprehensible, like Chinese'.[1] Chinese is now the most commonly spoken language in the world, but nearly two hundred years after its first performance the final movement of Opus 130 is still for many a difficult work to encounter.

Beethoven awaited news of the concert in a nearby tavern. If he had attended the first performance of Opus 130 on 21 March 1826 he would have observed the sort of response gratifying to most composers: such enthusiastic applause after two of the six movements that it prompted a spontaneous encore of each. The audience had appreciated the short second movement Scherzo with its suppressed scuttling rhythm and belligerently stamping middle section, and the genial *Alla tedesca* ('in the manner of a German Dance') fourth movement.[2] Beethoven scorned his audience's enthusiasm for the earlier music, however, concerned only with the response to the final movement: 'What, those trifles? Why not the fugue?'[3]

The Latin word *fuga* is the root of both *fugare* (to chase) and *fugere* (to flee). By 1825 the term 'fugue' was used to describe a wide range of imitative techniques. In a fugue a musical theme (the subject) is presented by one voice after another. As each new voice takes over the subject, those remaining are left free to manipulate the rhythmic, melodic and harmonic elements of the original subject, creating complex contrapuntal textures – the complete opposite of the homogeneous harmonies and rhythm that occur, for example, in the chorale of the *Heiliger Dankgesang*. The introduction of a counter-subject can further intensify the counterpoint. More than any other compositional technique, fugal writing brings to the fore the tension between independent voices that must cooperate. For Beethoven, acquiring fugal technique had therefore been an important element in learning how to compose chamber music.

Since his early studies in Vienna Beethoven had written fugues – indeed a fugue was recognised by Elector Maximilian Franz in Bonn as being the only genuinely new composition amongst the works that Haydn had sent to him in 1793 to demonstrate his student's progress. From 1794 Beethoven studied counterpoint with the composer, organist and theorist Johann Albrechtsberger, whom he saw as often as three times a week.[4] In addition to composing fugues himself, Beethoven arranged several by other composers for string quartet, including one from J. S. Bach's *Well-Tempered Clavier* and another from Handel's oratorio *Solomon*.[5] Beethoven would have known and perhaps played the viola part of Haydn's six Opus 20 quartets, composed in 1772, three of which end with fugues.

During the period that Beethoven worked on his Opus 18 quartets in 1799–1800, he wrote out in its entirety Mozart's String Quartet in G major, K387, the last movement of which begins with a fugal section. Shortly after I joined the Takács, I heard András repeatedly whistling a short motif as he wandered around an unfamiliar backstage area trying to find the dressing rooms. He explained that this was an accelerated version of the fugal theme from the last movement of K387 – a tune that the Hungarians whistled to track each other down amongst the disorienting settings of touring life.

The Opus 18 quartets contain many examples of lively imitative writing, but in the first movement of Opus 59, no. 1 Beethoven took the daring step of inserting a fugue into the already immensely long development section, a digression set in a remote key that probably increased the confusion of the quartet's first listeners. Beethoven changed some of the details in this fugue to such an extent that he had to sew a new piece of manuscript paper into the original autograph score.[6] In his *Grosse Fuge*, composed as the last movement of the string quartet Opus 130 – the last of the three written for Prince Galitzin – the form would exert a far more disruptive influence, dominating the whole final movement and dwarfing the movements that preceded it.

Beethoven began to think about Opus 130 while he worked on Opus 132 in Baden in May 1825. Over the course of the summer Opus 130 evolved into a six-movement work, the middle movements of which were of a shorter length more typically associated with a divertimento than a string quartet. As he contemplated how best to conclude Opus 130, Beethoven sketched over a dozen possible candidates for the main theme of the last movement, writing to Karl Holz on 24 August that he hoped his latest quartet would be completed by the end of the month.[7] The last movement became much longer than he had originally intended. Beethoven returned to Vienna from Baden in mid-October and did not finish the *Grosse Fuge* until the end of the year.

The composer described his latest fugue as 'sometimes free, sometimes strict'. It begins with the eight-note theme that will dominate the whole movement, played deliberately and *fortissimo* by the whole quartet. After an introduction full of stops and starts, Beethoven unleashes several minutes of unrelenting *fortissimo* dynamics in which a counter-subject featuring repeated dotted rhythms and violent melodic leaps competes with the main subject. During the first 158 bars these two themes are pitted against each other, an opening section of such violently argumentative nature as to take the genre quite beyond Goethe's definition of a string quartet as 'four rational people conversing with each other'.[8]

The following slow and lyrical section could not be more contrasting: smooth semiquavers are presented mainly in a *pianissimo* dynamic that offers a balm to the excesses of the first pages. The third and final section combines many different characters and dynamics, from its flippantly cheerful opening to wild and angry episodes, including an extraordinarily fast and difficult second-violin solo which Karl Holz, one of Beethoven's closest friends at this stage of his life but not an advocate of this fugue, might have found to be more a joke at his expense than a flattering commentary on his violinistic abilities.

Beethoven conjures up a level of emotional turmoil that can jeopardise the physical and mental control required to manage the considerable technical demands of the music. When Schuppanzigh's quartet began to rehearse Opus 130 in January 1826, they encountered difficulties throughout the piece and particularly with the *Grosse Fuge*. The composer attended their rehearsals, often sitting between the first and second violinists. According to Holz, Beethoven could hear well enough to give guidance on tempo and pacing: 'Often Schuppanzigh had quite a struggle with the difficult first violin part, at which Beethoven broke into peals of laughter.'[9] Holz doesn't report whether there was any such stumbling worthy of amusement in the execution of his own part, but as the piece was being prepared for publication in August 1826 he relayed a request from the publisher, Mattias Artaria, that Beethoven help the players by adding rehearsal letters to the *Grosse Fuge*: 'if they come apart or if things go badly, they can play it again starting from the letter.'[10]

According to the cellist in the New Hungarian Quartet, Andor Toth Jr, Dénes Koromzay once suggested that if the players ever lost their places in the fugue during a concert, he would 'accidentally' kick over his music stand, thus providing a less embarrassing reason to restart the piece than the loss of musical control. We have never yet come unstuck in a concert, but being far out of my comfort zone during a performance often means the fugue's motifs continue to whirl in my head late into the night, eroding sanity. The laws of imitative writing that govern a fugue may bind its elements together, but in the *Grosse Fuge* Beethoven imbues the individual lines with such fierce strength that dissonant harmonies and rhythmic tension seem at times to threaten the endeavour. Rational conversation is rejected in favour of the type of coruscating argument that may increase understanding even as it threatens the very foundations of a close relationship. The force unleashed is both potentially revitalising and destructive – not the sort of encounter one can easily experience every day.

Fortunately the unusual circumstances surrounding Opus 130 following its first performance have given me an excuse not to engage with the destabilising energy of its final movement too frequently. On 24 April 1826, a month after the audience had given the *Grosse Fuge* its first unenthusiastic reception, Mattias Artaria received the completed arrangement for four-hand piano that he had commissioned from the pianist Anton Halm. In August Artaria engraved the first edition of Opus 130 with its original last movement, the fugue, but he also enlisted Holz to persuade Beethoven to write another more accessible last movement, offering Beethoven a fee for the new finale and planning to publish the *Grosse Fuge* separately with its own opus number as Opus 133. According to Holz, Beethoven took only one day to agree to the plan: the question had perhaps already been on his mind since the unsuccessful first performance five months earlier. Beethoven did not deliver the alternative finale to Artaria until 22 November 1826. Completed only a few months before he died, it is a lighter and witty conclusion not only to Opus 130 but to his compositional output altogether: the last significant piece he completed before his death on 26 March 1827.[11]

Detractors of the new finale, feeling cheated of the heightened emotional drama offered by the *Grosse Fuge*, can explain Beethoven's decision to write another movement as the concession of someone weakened by illness, eager for the extra cash and shattered by Karl's suicide attempt just one month earlier. However, Beethoven was in no mood to make compromises that would weaken the effect of his music. Having initially dismissed his publisher's request to arrange the fugue for piano four hands as a menial task beneath his talents, Beethoven seized the project back from the pianist Anton Halm, incensed by Halm's revisions, which by reallocating some of the parts to make it easier for the players had in Beethoven's opinion weakened the impact of the piece.[12] Beethoven submitted his own four-hand version to Artaria in August 1826, around the same time that he agreed to write a new finale. His willingness to write an alternative to the *Grosse Fuge* suggests that, while defending the dramatic power of the original music, he was curious to explore another way of finishing a piece whose previous five movements embody such a wide range of characters and styles as to make a completely different ending an intriguing possibility.

*

After the actor Heinrich Anschütz complained about the alternative ending imposed by Austrian censors on the Burgtheater's 1822 version of Shakespeare's *King Lear*, he spent three days in jail for his outburst and was warned that further protests would result in him being fired.[13] Anschütz continued in the title role, outraged but probably not surprised by this so-called 'Viennese ending' in which both Lear and Cordelia survive. Historical dramas were particularly prone to the censor's interference; the collapse of rulers, murders and suicides were considered dangerously subversive subjects for the stages of the court theatres.[14]

Censorship was but one element in a comprehensive system of repression implemented by Emperor Franz I and Prince Metternich, Austria's most influential diplomat at the Congress of Vienna, whom the emperor appointed Chancellor of Austria in 1821. Franz had established a secret police force in Austria in 1793 that was charged with investigating threats to the Empire's security in the wake of the French Revolution. In August 1794 Beethoven witnessed the effects of this new force, whose discovery of a vague plot against the monarchy led to forty-five arrests, seven executions and many prison terms.

Foreigners were monitored with particular intensity throughout the Napoleonic Wars and during the Congress of Vienna, but after 1815 a network of informants from all walks of life, including valets, cab drivers, waiters and prostitutes, was instructed to focus on threats closer to home. Metternich was largely responsible for the creation of the Carlsbad Decrees of 1819, in which the German Federation, responding to student protests against conservative policies and the assassination of the playwright August von

Kotzebue, blacklisted all those teachers, writers and students in Germany and Austria who were suspected of holding liberal views. On 20 January 1820 the members of a group of Austrian students led by the poet Joseph Senn, which included the composer Franz Schubert, were arrested and their belongings searched. Senn was imprisoned for fourteen months and his academic career was ruined. Although there is no evidence that Schubert suffered more than a reprimand and a record of the incident in his police file, throughout his subsequent career he was plagued by the interference of censors. Both his operas and songs came under close scrutiny but Schubert assumed an unapologetic stance, continuing for example to compose large sections of music for his opera *Graf von Gleichen*, with its references to the bigamous activities of a noble, despite being warned by his friends of its likely ban.[15]

Moving in more aristocratic circles than Schubert, Beethoven was less vulnerable to the effects of the Carlsbad Decrees. Censorship did not generally impede his work, but the censor's refusal to allow the religious texts in the *Missa solemnis* to be performed at a secular concert led to Beethoven threatening to cancel the event, in which he also planned to include the first performance of the Ninth Symphony.[16] Only after the intervention of Count Moritz Lichnowsky (younger brother of Prince Lichnowsky), who wrote directly to the president of the police, did the censor back down. At the performance on 7 May 1824 the audience applauded and shouted 'Vivat!' so enthusiastically that the Police Commissioner yelled at them to remain silent.[17]

While the 'Ode to Joy' that concludes the Ninth Symphony was an idealistic political statement in its celebration of universal brotherhood, outside his music Beethoven was no political activist. His livelihood continued to be tied partially to the nobility, even if, as in the case of Princes Razumovsky and Galitzin, their straitened financial circumstances led to less reliable support. Furthermore the gradual democratisation of music production did not yet provide a dependable source of income. Beethoven was furious at the financial outcome of the 7 May concert featuring the Ninth Symphony: he expected a far greater sum than the net profit of 420 florins – an amount worth somewhat less than the 150 ducats that Prince Galitzin had promised the composer for three string quartets.

The *Grosse Fuge*, with its evocation of unruly individual voices and threat of chaos, if not an overt political statement, was at the least an uncanny harbinger of the spirit that would unleash violence and change throughout Europe in the revolutions of 1848. While Metternich did his utmost to maintain the political status quo, the censors focused their energies on excising from the Burgtheater such provocative material as plots portraying the downfall of kings. Those friends of Beethoven who had encouraged him to suppress the fugue primarily for artistic reasons were themselves products of a Viennese society where political conservatism went hand in hand with a preference for happier endings.

From behind the stage curtain sighs of disappointment were audible in the concert hall. 'I have some bad news,' the concert promoter had announced at the beginning of our concert for the Pittsburgh Chamber Music Society in September 2014. 'The Takács Quartet will *not* be playing the *Grosse Fuge* as the last movement of Opus 130 this

evening. Instead they will be playing Beethoven's alternative finale.' 'Why?' an audience member called out, her
exasperation shared by a reviewer of the concert who urged
the Society never again to accept Opus 130 in its revised
form.[18] We had been playing Opus 130 with its later finale
throughout the tour, but the movement listings for the
quartet in its original form had found their way into the
Pittsburgh concert programme. Even though the alternative finale had been written by the composer, not a later
censor, some listeners were outraged that we had deprived
them of a more emotionally satisfying conclusion. As we
continued to perform Opus 130 throughout the autumn,
we pondered how to heighten the impact of the revised
version, discussing not only the finale but also our interpretation of the previous movements.[19]

In May 1825, while Beethoven was convalescing in
Baden and working on Opus 132, he mentioned that Opus
130 would begin 'with a serious and heavy-going introduction'.[20] Eventually the opening slow music would come to
assume a more significant role. Following the introduction
an *Allegro* begins, only for its driving semiquaver rhythm
to be abruptly arrested. The slow music intrudes, an inva-
sive memory that will recur throughout the movement,
challenging the dominance of the *Allegro* sections.

Like two people who discover the essence of a disagreement only after preparatory skirmishes, the argument
between fast and slow comes to a head in the middle of the
movement. An *Allegro* that tries to leave behind the *Adagio*
music runs into more slow music after only one bar. The
Allegro tries once again with the same result. After a further three bars of *Adagio* an *Allegro* takes hold, but now the
second violin and viola repeat the same trance-like rhythm

and harmonies, rocking back and forth as if stunned by the insistent intrusions of slow music: a past memory paralysing the action of the present. A contemplative cello melody emerges from the stasis and is imitated by the first violin, both instruments playing high in their registers. Only after twenty-eight bars does the forceful momentum and virtuosic writing of the opening *Allegro* reassert itself.

Just before the end of the movement the argument recurs. Four consecutive bars alternate fast–slow–fast–slow. Beethoven is still weighing alternatives, returning to the conflict between the 'serious and heavy-going' atmosphere of the opening and the faster, more energetic music that follows. Although the fast eventually prevails, its exuberance is tamed: *pianissimo* echoes of the fast semiquaver passages that have dominated the movement propel the music towards a final cadence.

During two consecutive evenings at the Wigmore Hall in London we concluded our concert with Opus 130 with its alternative finale. Before the second concert we rehearsed onstage, proposing tweaks to the previous night's performance. In the first performance I thought we had successfully conveyed the exhilarating momentum in the driving *Allegro* sections. Geri and András felt that we had at times played the fast sections so precipitously as to leave no time for the sudden changes of dynamics back and forth between *forte* and *piano*. Karcsi mentioned that although several of our friends in the audience had enjoyed the performance, they observed afterwards in the Green Room that we sounded unsettled in the first movement. In order to convey the musical conflict, the contrasting elements would have to be conveyed more deliberately, not as if the performers were on the verge of losing control.

We rehearsed the opening bars of the next three movements, relatively short character pieces lacking the conflict inherent in the first movement, reminding each other to risk a more hushed yet manic *pianissimo* at the beginning of the second, and in the third to convey the conversational nature of the music by means of more visual contact as we passed a rising scale figure back and forth. In the genial fourth movement so appreciated by its first audience, Karcsi thought we were in danger of sounding sleepy: we applied faster bow speed and vibrato to inject more enthusiasm into the character.

We played the opening phrases of the Cavatina movement, a song that had, according to Holz, brought Beethoven to tears when he composed it. The version of the Cavatina recorded by the Budapest String Quartet was the last track on the Voyager Golden Record, one of several gold-plated discs placed on the Voyager probes launched by NASA in 1977 that were intended to convey a snapshot of humanity to any space traveller who might find it in the future.

'Do you think we're milking it too much?' Geri asked.

'Maybe it's lactose intolerant,' suggested Karcsi helpfully.

'I like the dark sound,' said András. 'It's not *pianissimo*, only *piano*. And *Adagio molto espressivo*.'

Beethoven had also marked the first bar *sotto voce* (to be played with a lowered voice or under the breath). As usual we addressed the inherent contradictions in Beethoven's instructions by sending someone out to listen in the hall. Karcsi leapt off the stage.

'Careful,' Geri said, laughing at his reckless acrobatics. 'We need you back here in one piece.'

'You don't need to push the sound,' Karcsi reported. The Wigmore acoustic aided a warm yet immediate sound with the minimum of effort. 'What's more disturbing, Ed, is the way you go up and down in the dynamics – I'm a bit seasick listening to you.' I tried again, playing with a more constant sound: there would be plenty of melodic disruption later in the movement.

Beethoven wrote *beklemmt* above my part in the middle section of the Cavatina that both Virginia and Leonard Woolf imagined as a suitable accompaniment to the exit of a coffin during a crematorium service. 'Oppressed', 'anguished' or 'constricted' are often offered as translations, but in this context perhaps 'afflicted' gets closest to the meaning. Above the weary yet ominous tread of a repeated rhythm in the three other parts, the first violin plays:

Rests choke the melodic line – the exact opposite of the smooth, *molto espressivo* phrases with which Beethoven began the movement. From a composer who expanded the range and intensity of emotional expression in his music comes another innovation and contradiction: grief too searing to be easily expressed, intended to be communicated to a public audience. There is no lonelier or more connecting moment in the whole Beethoven cycle.

Here in the *beklemmt* section I enjoy betraying elements of my training to serve the musical character. String players spend many hours practising how to draw a smooth bow over the string in order to make a sustained sound, but the sense of being afflicted, of having difficulty in expressing oneself, can be facilitated by a slightly unstable, quavering bow. To aid smooth shifting with the left hand, we are schooled to practise scales and arpeggios that cover the range of the instrument, memorising the geography of the fingerboard. But in this passage the hand can seem to flounder, fumbling its way up the D string as it tries to locate the next note. Although the impact of the fast music in the first movement may be reduced if the performers sound unsettled, a fragility in the player's execution can enhance the *beklemmt* character in the Cavatina.

At the opening of both the *Grosse Fuge* and its replacement finale Beethoven creates a link with the preceding music. Each begins on the same note with which the second violin finished the last chord of the Cavatina. The original fugue shatters the previously hushed mood with a dramatic unison G played by the whole group, whereas in the alternative finale the viola begins alone with a quietly buoyant quaver rhythm that sets the mood of the opening section.

In these two responses to the Cavatina lies the crux of the difference between the divergent versions. Anguished, defiant and browbeaten, the first sections of the fugue would serve well to convey King Lear's fractured state as he rages in a storm, grieving his betrayal at the hands of his two daughters, Goneril and Regan. Whereas the fugue violently wrests itself away from the Cavatina, the alternative finale tentatively picks up the pieces, like someone who after registering the ongoing anguish of a friend dares to suggest consolation. Because one function of the alternative finale is to reassemble, it seems to me especially important to exaggerate the sense of brokenness during the *beklemmt* passage. With the fugue to follow, the *beklemmt* section is a harbinger of catastrophe. In the alternative version the

Cavatina becomes the main emotional event of the piece, from which the finale retreats.

During our rehearsal at the Wigmore, Geri suggested that she start the alternative finale a little later than in previous concerts: continuing too hastily deprives the performers and audience of the silence that feels necessary both to register the solemn ending and to make a suspenseful connection to the next movement. During our performance that evening she extended the silence between the movements, lingering at the moment where Beethoven's plan for the end of Opus 130 had taken two separate paths.

Throughout his string quartet project Beethoven relished returning to his compositional choices to explore further possibilities. In 1801 he had implored his friend Amenda, to whom he had given his first version of Opus 18, no. 1, not to give it to anyone else as he had made some drastic changes. Many years later Beethoven revisited the fiery Trio section of that same piece by creating a more extreme version of his original idea in the third movement of Opus 127. Where previously only the first violinist was embroiled in fiendish passagework, in the later work the whole ensemble assumed a manic character. Similarly the recurrences of the slow introductory music in the first movement of Opus 130 are an expansion of an idea already presented many years previously in the last movement of his quartet Opus 18, no. 6, where the mysterious *Malinconia* introduction refuses to be pushed away by a more cheerful last movement. An even earlier example occurs in Beethoven's Piano Sonata in F minor, WoO 47, completed when Beethoven was only twelve or thirteen years old, in which the slow music of the introduction intrudes two-thirds of the way through the fast movement.

A year after finishing the original version of Opus 130, Beethoven went back to a fork in the road, composing musical themes closer to those he had initially sketched and discarded in favour of the *Grosse Fuge*, to produce the lighter final movement for Opus 130.[21] But the dramatic difference of style and content between these two last movements was more than an aberration inspired merely by the unique circumstances of that particular piece. In the nine months between completing the *Grosse Fuge* and writing his alternative finale Beethoven composed two more string quartets, Opus 131 and his last quartet, Opus 135. In both works he would continue to explore the problematic question of endings.

At the top of the last movement of Opus 135 Beethoven wrote an enigmatic inscription: *Der schwer gefasste Entschluss* ('The resolution reached with difficulty').[22] Underneath the title are two musical motifs; a question and an answer:

Muss es sein?

Es muss sein!   Es muss sein!

At the beginning of the slow introduction the viola and cello play the first motif in a low register: *Muss es sein?* ('Must it be?') The spare texture and mysterious mood are accentuated by the stark interval of a diminished fourth to which Beethoven set the last two words. The question is repeated with growing insistence as it reaches *fortissimo*, challenging tonality and demanding resolution.

The ensuing *Allegro* throws aside the ominous question with an exuberant answer – *Es muss sein!* – that sets the mood for most of the movement. When the question intrudes again later in the movement, a troublesome memory asserting itself with greater insistence, it is again left behind by an insouciant re-entry of the answering motif. The seemingly weighty and difficult question posed by the viola and cello at the opening of the movement is resolved by music of unbuttoned jollity.

Es muss sein! began its musical life as a humorous canon with the words, 'It must be! Yes, yes, yes, yes! Take out your wallet!' Throughout his life Beethoven created musical motifs, often of a satirical nature, for his friends and acquaintances, which could be sung or played as a canon – a straightforward technique in which each entrance usually imitates the previous one exactly, as in a round. Schuppanzigh was the victim of one such canon, the second part of which needs no translation: *Praise for the fat guy – Schuppanzigh ist ein Lump*. Beethoven's musical gifts were not always humorous: Dr Braunhofer had received the canon *Doctor, close the door 'gainst death* while Beethoven worked on Opus 132 in Baden.

Beethoven's friends offered several theories as to the source of inspiration for the *Es muss sein!* canon, including possible interchanges between Beethoven and his housekeeper, cook or publisher. Karl Holz provided the explanation most often quoted subsequently. An amateur musician, Ignaz Dembscher, had missed the first performance of Opus 130 in March 1826 and wanted to borrow the manuscripts from Beethoven in order to present another performance in his house. Beethoven refused to send him the parts unless Dembscher paid fifty florins as a retrospective payment – the rather steep price it would have cost him for a subscription ticket to the first performance. When Dembscher asked *Muss es sein?*, Holz reported, Beethoven wrote the four-part canon in reply.

Holz's story illuminates the gradual but significant change in music-making practices in the thirty years since Beethoven had composed his first chamber music in Vienna. The question of whether an amateur musician like Dembscher should pay a suitable subscription fee to present his own performance of Opus 130 would have seemed irrelevant twenty years earlier, in the setting of Prince Lichnowsky's or Count Razumovsky's private salon concerts. Whereas Beethoven's most significant early career developments were overseen by the Viennese nobility, by the end of his life publishers – and to a lesser extent subscribers through their purchase of concert tickets – provided Beethoven with a more significant if at times frustrating source of income.

As Beethoven worked on Opus 135 his friends continued their efforts to track down Prince Galitzin, who had still not paid Beethoven the agreed fee for Opus 132 and Opus 130. Although the irreverent tone of the *Es muss sein!* canon made it an unsuitable communication between Beethoven and his aristocratic patron, Prince Galitzin would have been its most worthy recipient: 'Yes, yes, yes, yes! Take out your wallet!' After Beethoven's death, his friends, most likely responding to Beethoven's wishes, dedicated Opus 135 to a more reliable and different type of supporter in the form of Johann Wolfmayer, a wealthy textile merchant who had for many years provided Beethoven with more discreet help than Princes Lichnowsky, Razumovsky and Galitzin – for example by surreptitiously replacing Beethoven's worn overcoat with a new one when he came to visit the composer.

If the *Es muss sein!* canon theme and inscription were initially inspired by financial matters, they took on a different significance within Beethoven's new quartet, according to a letter written by Beethoven to the publisher of Opus 135, Maurice Schlesinger:

> It has been difficult to compose this, because I was thinking of a much greater work. I composed it solely because I had promised it to you and needed the money. That it was difficult for me to do so you can gather from the '*Es muss sein*' ... Well that was a gruelling piece of work, in truth! Ugh, it is finished. Amen.[23]

In fact the letter was written not by Beethoven himself but by Schlesinger, who having apparently mislaid the original missive, wrote it down from memory more than thirty years later. In so far as Beethoven often finished his works under the pressure of missed deadlines, his communication with Schlesinger is plausible. This, however, would not be the last word on the meaning of the *Es muss sein!* motif at the core of this movement.

By adding to the finale of Opus 135 the title of *Der schwer gefasste Entschluss* and a serious musical setting of the *Muss es sein?* question (the canon had presented only the cheerful answer), Beethoven seemed to imbue it with philosophical significance. In his novel *The Unbearable Lightness of Being*, Milan Kundera saw a transformation of the humorous canon motif: 'By that time, Beethoven had forgotten about Dembscher's purse. The words *"Es muss sein!"* had acquired a much more solemn ring; they seemed to issue directly from the lips of Fate.'[24] Recent research on the sketches for the canon and quartet suggests that they may however have been composed at around the same time as each other, the mood of one more linked to the other than Kundera allows.[25] Furthermore, anyone listening to or playing the finale of Opus 135 would be unlikely to attribute the solemn weightiness to the *Es muss sein!* answer that Kundera assigns it. The resolution may be reached with difficulty, but when it arrives the mood is joyful and unencumbered.

Beyond Schlesinger's letter there is no record of Beethoven explaining the Opus 135 inscriptions. It is tempting to see the question and its answer as symbolising a progression in his attitude to life from a defiant refusal to bow to his misfortunes to an acceptance of his fate, but Beethoven would probably have ridiculed any such concrete explanation. Philosophical profundity may be implied, but the theme retains much of the high spirits and lightness of the original canon.

Whatever the significance of *Muss es sein?*, Beethoven was at this time fascinated by the compositional challenge of endings. Soon after he had completed the *Grosse Fuge* at the end of 1825 he had begun to work on Opus 131, a project that would occupy him throughout the first six months of 1826. In March he registered with disgust the audience's reaction to the first performance of Opus 130, disappointed that they had not reacted more favourably to the concluding *Grosse Fuge*. As he continued to work on Opus 131, Beethoven rejected his original scheme at the end of that piece for an eighth movement, entitled 'sweet song of rest'

– its opening melody would soon find a different resting place as the main melody of the slow movement of Opus 135. Instead, Beethoven finished off Opus 131 at the end of the seventh movement with a shockingly abrupt and brief conclusion.

It was in August 1826, while Beethoven worked on Opus 135, that he also agreed to write the alternative finale for Opus 130 to replace the *Grosse Fuge*. He finished Opus 135 in October. Even as he entitled the final movement of Opus 135 'The resolution reached with difficulty', Beethoven was contemplating how to provide a different ending to Opus 130: the finale was submitted to his publisher towards the end of November, an alternative if not a conclusive resolution to the problems posed by the *Grosse Fuge*.

While Beethoven's finale to Opus 130 was part of his larger experiment with endings, it also hinted at the emergence of a new compositional direction, one already explored in Opus 135. These are the only completed pieces of music that Beethoven left as evidence of an ambition to integrate lightness and weight, youthfulness and experience, comedy and tragedy, within more compact structures – all perhaps a response to the breadth and disorienting contrasts of some of his earlier works, including the *Grosse Fuge*.

'I hope still to bring forth into the world a few great works and then, like an old child, somewhere among good people to finish my earthly course.'[26] So Beethoven wrote from Vienna on 7 December 1826 to husband and wife Franz Wegeler and Eleonore von Breuning. It had taken Beethoven a year to reply to a letter from his old childhood friends from Bonn, who reproached him for not maintaining a correspondence, recalled happy shared scenes from their youth and entreated him to visit them at their home in Koblenz. In the last months of his life Beethoven took pains to rekindle the friendship, writing once again to Wegeler and arranging to send his old friends a shipment of wine. As Beethoven dreamed of an end to his life unburdened by difficult resolutions, he thought back to happier times spent in the company of childhood friends. By envisioning an 'old child' perhaps he meant to counter the deterioration in his health with a sense of lightened responsibility and humour.

Beethoven had returned to Vienna on 2 December from visiting his brother Johann. The composer was suffering from pneumonia, and although the attentions of Dr Wawruch averted immediate catastrophe, jaundice and dropsy set in, from which Beethoven never recovered. The last piece of music he wrote to have survived was a gloomy musical fragment included in a letter to Karl Holz in December 1826, not long after he completed the alternative finale. The canon accompanied the words: 'We all err, but each one in a different way.'[27] He was too unwell to realise his goal of composing new music in the first months of 1827 or even to participate in correcting the parts for the new finale of Opus 130, but the circumstances under which he spent his last months came close to fulfilling the wishes expressed in his letter to the von Breunings. Beethoven was visited by his closest friends in his spacious second-floor apartment in the centrally located Schwarzspanierhaus, which offered views of Vienna's church spires; beyond them were the trees of Vienna's largest park, the Prater, which Count Razumovsky had twenty years previously linked to his palace with a bridge and where Beethoven had spent many hours rambling and composing. It was a comfort to Beethoven to be living near another friend from his Bonn childhood, Stefan von Breuning, who visited frequently with his twelve-year-old son, Gerhard. Gerhard was an attentive and companionable boy who at one point noticed that Beethoven was plagued by bedbugs and organised a change of bedding. Other visitors included Beethoven's brother Johann, his personal assistant Anton Schindler, Karl Holz and the publisher Tobias Haslinger. Beethoven's nephew Karl left Vienna on 2 January to embark upon the military career he had threatened Beethoven with several years earlier. But even this conflicted relationship had reached a resolution of sorts. Shaken by Karl's attempted suicide – at that time considered a crime – Beethoven was desperate for any solution that would save his nephew from the authorities. He changed the dedication of Opus 131 to Baron von Stutterheim to thank the Baron for accepting Karl into his regiment.

In 1874 Gerhard van Breuning published his book *Memories of Beethoven*, in which he described Beethoven's physical environment at the end of his life:

> To the left of the head of the bedstead was a bedside table and further along, towards the stove, a long table. Next to the bed was a small table with two or three chairs for the few friends who came to visit him. On the bedside table stood a black japanned box in which he kept his cash; on the floor alongside the bedside table, a little yellow folding writing desk.[28]

In March 1827, less than a week before he died, Beethoven wrote to the banking firm Stieglitz and Co., still trying to track down the money owed to him by Prince Galitzin.

Beethoven requested that the much-needed money be transferred to his account and the terms of the contract finally fulfilled.[29] Not until 1858, the year Beethoven's nephew Karl died from liver disease at the age of fifty-two, did Galitzin's son George deposit the outstanding amount into a German account to be used by Beethoven's remaining heir, Karl's widow. It is unclear whether she ever received the money.[30]

During his last three months Beethoven had several bouts of abdominal surgery to drain fluid from his failing body, and throughout February and early March he continued to entertain some hope of recovery. But a few days before he died at the age of fifty-six, Beethoven made an announcement to his visitors: *Plaudite amici, finita est comedia* ('Applaud friends, the comedy is finished').

In Franz Grillparzer's funeral oration for Beethoven – delivered by Heinrich Anschütz, the Burgtheater's King Lear – the Austrian writer and dramatist neatly summed up the contradictory forces at work in Beethoven's music:

> From the cooing of doves to the rolling of thunder, from the craftiest interweaving of well-weighed expedients of art to that awful pitch where planful design disappears in the lawless whirl of contending natural forces he had traversed and grasped it all.[31]

Grillparzer could have been describing the impact of the *Grosse Fuge* on its first listeners, where 'planful design disappears in the lawless whirl of contending natural forces' – the alternative finale offering a 'well-weighed' alternative.

Beethoven died in surroundings much as he had

imagined in his last letter to the von Breunings. But in his two endings to Opus 130 the ambivalences and contradictions that dominate his late style came to a head. Nearly two hundred years later passionate preferences for one or the other reaffirm the dualistic tendencies of his art and present a dilemma that can never be entirely resolved.

At Zellerbach Hall on the University of California's Berkeley campus, Geri begins the alternative finale and we embark upon Beethoven's final music as if there were no other choice. In rehearsal we investigate different interpretative options but during a concert there is no time to regret rejected options. And yet the presence of the fugue hovers over Opus 130, guiding our interpretation of its successor.

Comparing the openings of each provides clues as to which aspects we should characterise most vividly. In the introductory section of the *Grosse Fuge*, after a single *forte* G played by everyone, the subject enters *fortissimo*, all four parts in unison. After a silence the subject tries again, another unison now sweeping forward in a faster rhythm. But after only two bars, silence again intrudes. The same dichotomy is repeated: subject followed by silence. Then the first violin enters quietly, a hushed after-tremor to the original theme, taken over by the cello, while above enter tentative fragments of commentary, the voices separate and uncertain. The first violin is left alone, rudderless, playing the opening theme *pianissimo*. Rests choke each note – another *beklemmt* musical phrase in all but name. Finally the first violin shatters its own mood, beginning the fugue itself *fortissimo* and joined in quick succession by viola, second violin and cello: four voices that pull and push against each other, denying the homogeneity of the opening, chasing and fleeing the very material that binds them together.

During the opening twenty-five bars of the alternative finale, dynamic and rhythmic contrasts are minimised. The regular quaver motion with which the viola begins continues to supply an unwavering pulse, supporting a graceful, tidy theme that brushes off the sadness of the Cavatina. Occasional hairpin dynamics louder and softer provide the only variation to an otherwise constant *pianissimo* dynamic. As one player takes over the quaver accompaniment another takes a turn playing the tune. There is no tension between the lines here but rather lively yet hushed cooperation. Even in Zellerbach's two-thousand-seat auditorium we risk sustaining the extended *pianissimo* as an opposite to the desperate opening cry of the fugue we are not playing. Countering the chasm-like breaks that fracture the beginning of the *Grosse Fuge*, we play its alternative with as constant a pulse as possible, Geri's quaver figure supplying effortless and inevitable momentum.

The opening sections of this finale may escape the strife of the original version, but in the middle of the movement Beethoven seems briefly to recall the violent contrasts of the fugue. Karcsi and I begin a fugal section quietly, joined by Geri and András. The contrapuntal argument escalates until we land together on a *fortissimo* unison passage, hammering out the notes of that most unstable of chords, a diminished seventh, in the continuous quaver rhythm that has driven the movement since its opening. We kindle this conflagration with rougher-sounding bow-strokes than usual, and I wonder if Beethoven intended this passage for that first unenthusiastic audience who rejected the fugue: even in this 'nicer' finale they will have to contend with one violent outburst.

If this section seems briefly reminiscent of the *Grosse Fuge*, the manner in which Beethoven leaves it behind is a transition of mood already accomplished in his previous quartet, Opus 135. Two-thirds of the way through its finale, the anxious intensity of the last *Muss es sein?* question evaporates in an instant, replaced by the tongue-in-cheek return of the canon theme. Similarly in the Opus 130 finale our belligerent quavers change from *fortissimo* to *pianissimo* in just a few seconds, setting up a return of the quietly cheerful theme with which the movement began. We turn the corner with the slightest relaxing of the tempo, giving a fraction more space to change our sound; rough, heavy bow-strokes near the bridge are replaced by more springing and brushed strokes over the fingerboard.

Sudden juxtapositions of mood are nothing new in Beethoven's quartets, but here there is a sense of weightier emotions being sloughed off, contrasts no longer threatening to the unity of the work. The movement reminds me of a couple who argue fiercely, secure in the knowledge that soon enough laughter will follow. Knowing that it is Beethoven's last completed work, I find it hard not to imbue this movement with an extra-musical significance similar to that sometimes attributed to Opus 135. The battles of the *Grosse Fuge* have been fought and, if not resolved, at least superseded. Now there is little more to be done: for the old child the comedy is nearly over – *Es muss sein!* But Beethoven was no stranger to serious illness and was eager 'to create a few more great works' before he died. It seems unlikely he viewed the finale as his epitaph. As well as being an alternative ending to Opus 130, the finale along with Opus 135 represents a new beginning, a compositional direction that Beethoven would perhaps have explored further if he had had time to develop the few existing sketches for a new string quintet and tenth symphony.

When I first played through the last page of this first violin part such speculations were far from my mind. I laughed out loud at the ludicrously difficult writing with its passages of busy semiquavers that refuse to arrange themselves in one register or on one string, requiring facile leaps with the left hand and frantic oscillations with the right. Poor Schuppanzigh: what a sting in the tail for the rotund elder statesman, trying to keep younger violinists at bay and reclaim his reputation after the debacle of Opus 127!

The ending of this generally more palatable and digestible finale is uncomfortable for the players. Whereas the exhilarating resolution of the *Grosse Fuge* is achieved organically from a build-up of dynamics and rhythmic energy that unfurls into the last cadence, in the alternative finale scurrying semiquavers land on an uncomfortable pause, pulling up at the edge of a precipice. Now we must seize two chords out of nowhere, a physically awkward change of technique that often does not come off exactly as I would like. When in this performance I mangle the crisp execution of bow-stroke across all four strings, the notes speak unclearly and there is no chance for us to end with a clean attack. Nonetheless the Berkeley audience applauds enthusiastically and my moment of imprecision is forgotten – at least until our next rehearsal.

Would Beethoven have derided listeners nearly two hundred years later for applauding this alternative finale, as he did his first audience for rejecting the *Grosse Fuge*? I doubt it. We have not given our audience a choice; if there's anyone to castigate it is the performers. The problem of the two endings is as frustrating for us as it is for some audience members. We spend so much time and energy seeking to combine disparate elements in Beethoven's string quartets, and yet here at the conclusion of Opus 130 there is no way simultaneously to convey the vastly differing impact of both endings. An innovative concert promoter could return the choice to the audience by furnishing them with an electronic voting machine – of course designed by independent contractors not funded by backers of either ending. At a predetermined moment the audience would vote on their preferred conclusion, the result flashing up on the music stands to be implemented by the players. Even this approach might seem to betray Beethoven's often mistrustful relationship with his audiences: given the opportunity perhaps he would jump up from his seat and demand the rejected version.

After our Berkeley performance I imagine Beethoven coming backstage to point out an unsuccessful bow-stroke or tempo choice. *Why have you not played my fugue for over five years? Do you think it not worthy of your attention?* Under his persistent questioning I cannot deny that I have been avoiding the *Grosse Fuge*, hiding behind an alternative ending less taxing to muscles and psyche. When I first learned Opus 130 I had more zest for the fugue's violent energy, but now I am drawn to the music of Opus 135's *Es muss sein!* or Opus 130's alternative finale, which dare to brush off past conflicts and anguish.

Dramatic portrayals of a string quartet necessarily focus on crisis and conflict, the *Grosse Fuge* a more apt soundtrack to their stories than the alternative finale. At the end of Michael Hollinger's gripping drama, *Opus*, the smashing of a violin epitomises the group's strife. In the film *A Late Quartet* the first violinist finds an efficient way to spark hostility with two of his quartet colleagues by starting an affair with their daughter. While such melodrama is not outside the realm of possibility, the members of a string quartet who work together for a long time choose for the most part to let go of the inevitable tensions or strains of working so closely together. Unlike in some kinds of reality show, the aim is to keep four people on the island. By electing to take the approach of an alternative finale that lightly moves away from suffering, music rather than personalities can become the dominant story.

Karcsi, Geri and András have been my dear partners in this intimate endeavour for the last decade. In order to maintain an enjoyable working environment we all practise a degree of emotional restraint, filtering our thoughts and feelings as we gauge what is best left unsaid. Every now and again we experience a *Grosse Fuge* of sparky interactions that while leaving us briefly raw and vulnerable allow a return to the daily cheer of the alternative finale. Keeping the peace is something I value now much more than I did twenty years ago – at least that's my sense of it. A first violinist's narrative cannot be fully trusted and as with all aspects of this story, my colleagues might tell it in a different way. Nonetheless the *Grosse Fuge* does not appeal to me in the same way that it did when I first joined the quartet. After more than twenty years playing in the Takács I have more to lose now than I did then, and perhaps my attitude marks an increased emotional conservatism.

All the more reason for Beethoven to deride me! What business do I have censoring his works for my own needs? The fugue demands to be played, like so much of

Beethoven's great music not merely affirming but challenging a life view or emotional state, not allowing one to stand still. It provides and requires an artistic liberalism that will always be safe from the likes of Prince Metternich.

When we play the Beethoven cycle we conclude the first concert with Opus 130 and its alternative finale. We play the piece again to finish the last concert, this time with the *Grosse Fuge* having the final say, its extreme demands and rewards making it the most suitable conclusion to the Beethoven quartet journey.

How shall we address its particular challenges when we next rehearse it? Beethoven composed one hundred and twenty-eight bars of continuous *fortissimo*, but an indiscriminate application of our loudest dynamic will at times make it hard to hear the independent lines. Perhaps we should modify our dynamics to highlight specific melodic shapes. If only we could ask Beethoven's advice, for he might find our accommodations as unsatisfying as the blandishing alterations of the pianist and arranger Anton Halm: perhaps the composer would insist that we create as much cacophony as possible.

Even though there are no conclusive answers to such interpretative questions, when we next rehearse the fugue Beethoven will lurk in the background, sometimes coming forward to beat time or revise a dynamic marking in his score, occasionally snatching one of our instruments to demonstrate a bow-stroke. Often he is brusque, intolerant of any imperfections or uncertainties in our playing. Now he sits down between the two violinists, momentarily subdued, straining to translate what his ears distort into the ideal sounds he imagines. The first violinist miscounts and skips his entrance, confused by relentless syncopated entrances that challenge the basic pulse. Beethoven jumps to his feet, arms outstretched, head thrown back, roaring with laughter as he urges us to try again.

Behind our conversations, choices and revaluations of his music lies Beethoven's questioning spirit, with which he already began to challenge his father from an early age. 'What stupid stuff are you scratching at now?' Johann van Beethoven interrupted his son's violin practice: 'You know that I cannot stand that. Scratch on the notes, or you'll never get anywhere.' The young boy continued to make up tunes on the violin, to the annoyance of his father, who reprimanded him for dabbling in composition prematurely and urged him instead to work hard on the clavier and violin. As it had been for Mozart, improvisation was a natural way for the precocious composer to express himself. Although Beethoven's father admonished him, he recognised his son's unusual gift: 'When you've learned enough then you can and you will play from your head. But don't try it now. You're not ready for it.'[32]

Beethoven's earliest composition, published in 1783 when he was twelve years old, was a set of nine variations for solo piano on a march by Ernst Christoph Dressler. A theme in a minor key was at that time an unusual choice of material for a set of variations, the mood surprisingly serious for the work of a boy. The dotted rhythm, alongside the key, lends it the character of a funeral march. Beethoven possibly intended the piece as a memorial to his second cousin, the talented violinist Franz Rovantini, who lived with the Beethoven family in Bonn for several years, gave Beethoven violin lessons and died after a sudden illness at the age of twenty-four.[33] Although each variation ends abruptly, Beethoven achieves a sense of progression by means of a gradual acceleration of note values and increasingly virtuosic writing for the piano. After eight variations that exactly follow the harmonies of the theme, the jubilant final section is in C major, the funeral march left far behind by cascades of sparkling scales.

The variation form that would become so significant in his exploratory late style provided Beethoven with a natural outlet for both his early compositional experiments and his talent for improvisation on the piano. In November 1791 the composer and author Carl Ludwig Junker recalled giving Beethoven a theme on which to improvise variations and was taken with the combination of virtuosity, expressivity and a seemingly inexhaustible supply of ideas that the unassuming young man offered. Compared to another contemporary pianist, Junker found Beethoven 'more eloquent, meaningful and expressive – in short, he speaks to the heart. He is thus as good a player of *Adagios* as he is of *Allegros*.'[34]

In the last of twenty-four variations composed by the twenty-one-year-old composer in 1791 on a theme by the Italian operatic composer Vincenzo Righini, runs of cheerful semiquavers suggest another triumphant resolution like that of the Dressler Variations, but here a digression into a slower *Allegro* and disorienting shifts of key ensure that the path becomes teasingly indirect. An accelerating *Allegro* followed by a *Presto assai* rekindles the hope of a joyful end, like carefree children running off to play having survived a parental admonition. But Beethoven saves his most radical idea for last. The note values become slower and slower, the dynamic fades to *pianissimo*, the chirpy energy of the original theme is finally dissolved and the piece ends with a simple chord, intro-spection trumping cheerfulness and virtuosity. Beet-hoven's childhood friend Gottfried Fischer had observed a spirit of inward musing in a boy who was happiest when he was alone, while his sister Cäcilie remembered Beet-hoven staring into space and unwilling to explain what was on his mind.[35] Beethoven's early ability to convey pri-vate speculation in his music was one of the qualities that spoke to his audiences.

Introspection was not the characteristic that the horn player Nikolaus Simrock (who later set up a publishing house in Bonn) remarked upon when he heard his friend perform the piece in the autumn of 1791. Simrock admired his 'daintiness and brilliant lightness', noting that Beet-hoven spontaneously added a couple of new variations to his already memorised performance.[36] Beethoven's subse-quent success in establishing himself in Vienna as a pianist–composer owed much to his instinctive ability to combine different elements: crowd-pleasing virtuosity went hand in hand with meditative playing, both presented with a sense that the music was being invented in the moment.

Anyone who engages with Beethoven's music – as an audience member or a professional or amateur string quar-tet player – is a lucky custodian of his restless, enquiring spirit. Whether we embark upon the slow movement of Opus 18, no. 1 with its revised character instruction, *affetu-oso ed appassionato*, or begin to play for the unexpected sec-ond time the Trio section with its Russian theme in Opus 59, no. 2, or launch into the cheeky *Marcia* that Beethoven eventually selected to follow the *Heiliger Dankgesang*, I imagine the moment of decision when Beethoven sat at a desk in his lodgings or wandered through his favourite forests of the Helenenthal outside Baden and chose between one path and another.

In our studio at the University of Colorado, just across the courtyard from where I first auditioned with the Takács, a young ensemble named the Altius Quartet, in 2015 our Graduate Quartet in Residence, open their music for the first movement of Opus 131. They are a talented group with some concerts and competition successes and many hours of rehearsal experience behind them – it's a good time for them to tackle Opus 131. They describe the same feelings of confusion and awe when they first read the whole piece through that I still remember from my first encounter. I ask them what issues have come up during their initial rehearsals. They describe the challenge in the opening movement of achieving a sufficiently serious and melancholy character without the music sounding turgid – the same question we investigated when we last tackled the piece at the Wigmore Hall several years previously and one to which they will in due course fashion their own answers. When they begin to play I admire how quickly they convey a sense of loneliness in their individual statements of the theme while nonetheless beginning a conversation as they hand the opening fugal phrase to one another.

The members of the Altius Quartet are at the beginning of their exploration of this music just as I was when I joined the Takács over twenty years ago. However long one has been grappling with Beethoven's quartets, sustaining a sense of discovery is as critical to conveying the spirit of the music as it is to sustaining any close relationship. When I return to a Beethoven quartet I like to remind myself of a young boy's early challenges to his father and the shocked first reactions of audiences and players to Beethoven's music. Often I recall the early days of the founding members of the Takács Quartet, of whose artistic identity I am so fortunate to have become part. Their adventurous spirit and willingness to take a chance on a young Englishman with much to learn inspires me all these years later.

I imagine them on a small field at the side of the Autobahn – four Hungarian men in their early twenties, revelling in the chance to stretch their legs after many hours' driving. Two Russian-made Ladas loaded down with luggage are parked near the temporary soccer field. They stand in a circle, instrument cases next to them, kicking a football to and fro. There is an easy camaraderie in their interactions as they try to break their record for the number of passes executed without the ball touching the ground, like a musical phrase passed from one to the next, buoyant, vital and expectant. Now they consult maps, arguing about the choice of route – a string quartet will always find something to debate – and squeeze instrument cases and players into cars. Luggage piled high, rear-view mirrors obscured, they press forward, hoping to complete their long journey west before nightfall.

Acknowledgements

To Karcsi, Geri and András I am immeasurably grateful for providing years of companionship, support, humour, wisdom and fulfilling music-making. Without them this book would have been out of the question. My attempts to portray their lively, compassionate personalities are bound to fall short, while my narrative of the quartet's story is entirely my own, and is as such necessarily one-sided. The dialogue from rehearsals is my best attempt to capture the spirit of our conversations rather than a word-for-word rendition. Any errors or inaccuracies are my own. Roger Tapping and Gábor Ormai's company and musicianship were immensely important to me during my formative years in the group, and I thank Gábor Takács-Nagy for the inspiring example he set me. My narrative leaves out much of the first eighteen years of the quartet's history before I joined the group when the founding members established their international career. During that time I was a student and remain especially grateful to my teachers: Howard Davis (first violinist of the Alberni Quartet), Felix Andrievsky, Dorothy DeLay and Piotr Milewski.

In addition to our General Manager Christa Phelps and North American Manager Seldy Cramer, both of whose dedication has changed our lives for the better, too many other friends, local managers and concert promoters have provided support and encouragement for me to list them all. Chris and Margot Brauchli, Harry Campbell, Chris and Barbara Christoffersen, Nancybell Coe, Christina Daysog,

Robert Cole, Simon Eadon, Amelia Freedman, John Gilhooly, Georges Gara, Ara Guzelimian, Judith Glyde, Peter and Diana Held, Norma R. Johnson, Gary and Judy Judd, Andrew Keener, John Kongsgaard, Oswald Lehnert, William Lyne, Ian Malkin, Alexander and Thais Mark, Evans Mirageas, Jane Moss, Paul Nelson, Ed and Liz Newlands, Betty Perkins, Simon Perry, Chris Pope, John and Doreen Ruddock, Daniel and Boyce Sher, Asadour Santourian, Adele and Julia Schottlander, Kathy Shuman, Chuck Speers, Dickon Stainer, William Starr, Matiás Tarnopolsky and Eric Wilson deserve special mention. The daughters of Fay Shwayder, Susan de Jong and Judy Drake, have continued the generous instrument loan agreement initiated by their mother. Over the years the quartet has been indebted to a number of wonderful players who helped us out during the difficult periods when one or other of us was incapacitated. We benefitted from the musicianship of violinists Lina Bahn, Alexander Kerr and Peter Salaff and violists Erika Eckert, Zoltán Tóth and Louise Williams. Annamaria Karacson, Katalin Boros and Tom Walther have provided support in so many ways, not only in their capacity as quartet spouses.

This book was the idea of my imaginative agent, Rebecca Carter, who set me a number of canny homework assignments several years ago until the project began to take shape. Belinda Matthews at Faber aided the evolution of the book with her enthusiasm for the concept and her expert guidance in balancing its different elements. Thanks to Michael Downes for his astute reading and copyediting of the text and to Samantha Matthews for preparing the book for publication.

Richard Beales facilitated my first writing assignment,

while I have also benefitted from the advice and expertise of his father, historian Derek Beales. Special thanks to James Brody, Daniel Chua, Bruce Holsinger, Alan Johnson, Robert McDonald, Dick and Marjorie McIntosh, Martie McMane, Joshua Robinson, Paul and Sheila Russell, Ittai Shapira and Blair Singer. Seldy Cramer and David Lawrence Morse generously provided comprehensive feedback on the manuscript in its various forms, as did my brother Martin Dusinberre and parents William and Juliet Dusinberre.

Sam Dusinberre kindly shared his software expertise by preparing the musical examples. In addition to her wisdom and patience, and countless hours spent helping me, my wife Beth Dusinberre provided translation advice. To Beth and Sam, thanks for everything, including conversation around the dinner table on subjects even more riveting than violin strings.

Notes

Prologue: Opus 131

1. W. von Lenz, *Eine Kunst-Studie* (Kassel, 1855–60) 1:216f, quoted in Lewis Lockwood, *Beethoven: The Music and the Life* (New York, 2003), p. 442.
2. Alexander Wheelock Thayer, *Thayer's Life of Beethoven*. Revised and edited by Elliot Forbes, 2 vols (Princeton, NJ, 1964), vol. 1, p. 409, reproduced with permission of Princeton University Press.
3. *Briefwechsel*. Edited by Sieghard Brandenburg, 7 vols (Munich 1996–8), vol. 2, no. 585. *The Letters of Beethoven*. Translated and edited by Emily Anderson, 3 vols (London, 1961), vol. 1, no. 376, reproduced with permission of Palgrave Macmillan. (References are given only to the *Briefwechsel*, unless I am directly quoting Anderson's translation. Translations are taken from the Anderson edition except where noted otherwise. I have used only the letters translated by Anderson which also appear in the more recent Brandenburg edition.)
4. I am grateful to Daniel Chua for sharing his thoughts some years ago about the provisional nature of endings in Beethoven's late quartets.

1. Audition: Opus 59, no. 3

1. Joseph Kerman, 'Beethoven Quartet Audiences', in Robert Winter and Robert Martin (eds), *The Beethoven Quartet Companion* (Berkeley, CA, 1994), p. 16. As Kerman says, the source of the anecdote is unclear but the sentiment is consistent with the demands Beethoven placed on his musicians.
2. *Briefwechsel*, vol. 1, no. 182. Anderson, vol. 1, no. 92.
3. *Briefwechsel*, vol. 1, no. 67. Anderson, vol. 1, no. 53.
4. Theodore Albrecht (ed.), *Letters to Beethoven and Other Correspondence*, 3 vols (Lincoln, NE, 1996), vol. 1, no. 13.

5. *Briefwechsel*, vol. 1, no. 67. Anderson, vol. 1, no. 53.

6. http://de.wikisource.org/wiki/Heiligenstädter_Testament, accessed 9 April 2015.

7. Quoted in Barry Cooper, *Beethoven* (Oxford, 2000), p. 175.

2. Joining the Quartet: Opus 18, no. 1

1. Baron Riesbeck, *Travels Through Germany, in a Series of Letters,* translated by Paul Henry Maty (London, 1787), p. 309.

2. Riesbeck, pp. 239–40.

3. John Owen, *Travels Into Different Parts of Europe, in the Years 1791 and 1792*, 2 vols (London, 1796), vol. 2, p. 466.

4. Owen, vol. 2, p. 487.

5. For a nuanced discussion of the decline of *Hauskapelle* see Tia DeNora, *Beethoven and the Construction of Genius* (Berkeley, CA, 1995), pp. 40–4.

6. Daniel Heartz, *Mozart, Haydn and Early Beethoven* (New York, 2009), p. 223.

7. Riesbeck, p. 243.

8. Albrecht, vol. 1, no. 16.

9. Franz Wegeler and Ferdinand Ries, *Beethoven Remembered* (Arlington, VA, 1987), p. 32. In his account, Wegeler misremembered the instruction, recalling that Beethoven in fact asked for the passage to be played on the *G* string, but he was clearly mistaken.

10. Wegeler and Ries, p. 75.

11. Wegeler and Ries, p. 36.

12. *Briefwechsel*, vol. 1, no. 17. Anderson, vol. 1, no. 12.

13. Charles Ingrao, *The Habsburg Monarchy* (Cambridge, 2000), p. 225.

14. *Briefwechsel*, vol. 1, no. 17. Anderson, vol. 1, no. 12.

15. *Briefwechsel*, vol. 1, no. 20. Anderson, vol. 1, no. 16.

16. Ingrao, p. 231.

17. For an interesting profile on Koromzay, see Judith Glyde, 'Quarter of a Legend', in *The Strad*, vol. 108, no. 1283 (London, 1997).

18. Cooper, p. 88.

19. Cooper, p. 45.

20. *Briefwechsel*, vol. 1, no. 42. Beethoven wrote this note on a copy of the first violin part.

21. *Briefwechsel*, vol. 1, no. 43.
22. Cooper, p. 86.
23. Albrecht, vol. 1, no. 31.
24. *Briefwechsel*, vol. 1, no. 67. Anderson, vol. 1, no. 53.
25. *Briefwechsel*, vol. 1, no. 65. Anderson, vol. 1, no. 51.
26. The instruments are now on display at the Beethovenhaus in Bonn.
27. Thayer, ed. Forbes, vol. 1, p. 265.
28. *Briefwechsel*, vol. 1, no. 67.
29. Quoted in Christina Bashford, 'The string quartet and society', in Robin Stowell (ed.), *The Cambridge Companion to the String Quartet* (Cambridge, 2003), p. 4.
30. *Briefwechsel*, vol. 1, no. 67.
31. Thayer, ed. Forbes, vol. 1, p. 26.

3. Fracture: Opus 59, no. 2

1. Quoted in Thayer, ed. Forbes, vol. 1, p. 375.
2. Henry Reeve, *Journal of a Residence at Vienna and Berlin, in the Eventful Winter 1805–6* (London, 1877), p. 46.
3. Reeve, p. 55.
4. Reeve, p. 65.
5. Reeve, p. 79.
6. Translation of both folk songs by Laura J. Olson.
7. For an interesting theory about the inclusion of an additional folk song in Opus 59, no.3, see Mark Ferraguto, 'Russianness and Learned Style in the "Razumovsky" String Quartets', in *Journal of the American Musicological Society*, vol. 67, no. 1 (Berkeley, CA, 2014).
8. Robert Coughlan, *Elizabeth and Catherine: Empresses of All the Russias* (New York, 1974), p. 39.
9. Alan Tyson, 'The Razumovsky Quartets: Some Aspects of the Sources', in Alan Tyson (ed.), *Beethoven Studies 3*, (New York, 1973), pp. 128–30.
10. Thayer, ed. Forbes, vol. 1, p. 403.
11. At some point Beethoven considered changing the dedication of the Opus 59s to Lichnowsky, perhaps hoping to patch up their

relationship. See Tyson, p. 134.

12. Joseph Kerman, *The Beethoven Quartets* (New York, 1967), p. 130.

13. Quoted in Thayer, ed. Forbes, vol. 1, p. 409. This reference includes the reactions of both Romberg and Radicati to the Opp. 59s.

14. *The Critical Reception of Beethoven's Compositions by his German Contemporaries*, 2 vols, ed. Wayne M. Senner, Robin Wallace and William Meredith (Lincoln, NE, 1999), vol. 2, pp. 97–8.

15. Leo Tolstoy, *The Kreutzer Sonata*, translated by Isai Kamen (New York, 2003), pp. 59–61.

16. Quoted in Thayer, ed. Forbes, vol. 1, pp. 206–7.

17. Tyson, p. 120.

18. Maria Razumovsky, *Die Razumovskys, Eine Familie am Zarenhof* (Cologne, 1998), p. 184.

19. Thayer, ed. Forbes, vol. 1, p. 401.

20. Sir Robert Adair, *Historical Memoir of a Mission to the Court of Vienna in 1806* (London, 1844), p. 13.

21. Anton Felix Schindler, *Beethoven As I Knew Him: A Biography*, edited by Donald W. MacArdle, translated by Constance S. Jolly (Chapel Hill, NC, 1966), p. 60. Reproduced with permission of the University of North Carolina Press, www.uncpress.unc.edu.

22. Quoted in Thayer, ed. Forbes, vol. 1, pp. 408–9.

23. *Briefwechsel*, vol. 2, no. 392. Anderson, vol. 1, no. 220.

24. http://www.raptusassociation.org/op74_e.html. Translation of *Allgemeine musikalische Zeitung*, no. 21, 11 May 1811 (Leipzig), Columns 348–51, last accessed 31 March 2015.

25. *Briefwechsel*, vol. 3, no. 983.

26. Thayer, ed. Forbes, vol. 1, p. 561.

27. Schindler, ed. MacArdle, p. 169.

28. Schindler, ed. MacArdle, p. 205.

29. Schindler, ed. MacArdle, p. 174.

30. August De La Garde-Chambonas, *Anecdotal Recollections of the Congress of Vienna*, translated by Maurice Fleury (London, 1902), p. 257.

31. Hilde Spiel (ed.), *The Congress of Vienna: An Eyewitness Account*, translated by Richard H. Weber (Philadelphia, 1968), p. 133.

32. Ludwig van Beethoven, *Konversationshefte*, 11 vols (Leipzig, 1972–2001), ed. Karl-Heinz Köhler, Grita Herre and Dagmar Beck, vol. 10, p. 75.

33. *Konversationshefte*, vol. 10, p. 71.
34. *Konversationshefte*, vol. 10, p. 70.
35. Countess Lulu Thürheim, *Mein Leben: Erinnerungen aus Österreichs grosser Welt 1788–1819*, 4 vols (Munich, 1913), vol. 4, p. 112.

4. Re-creation: Opus 127

1. Friedrich Reichardt quoted in Robert Winter, 'Quartets in Their First Century', in *Beethoven Quartet Companion*, p. 37.
2. After the Beethoven recordings we moved to the recording company Hyperion, with whom we have recorded at least one disc a year since 2005.
3. The recordings were made possible by the support of many subscribers including Gary and Judy Judd (daughter of Harry Campbell) and Norma R. Johnson. The complete list of supporters can be found in the relevant CD booklets.
4. *Briefwechsel*, vol. 4, nos. 1468 and 1478.
5. Cooper, p. 347.
6. Albrecht, vol. 2, no. 290.
7. Albrecht, vol. 2, no. 295.
8. For the background to the first performances of Opus 127, I am indebted to two articles: Robert Adelson, 'Beethoven's String Quartet in E Flat Op. 127: A Study of the First Performances' in *Music and Letters*, vol. 79, no. 2 (Oxford, 1998), pp. 219–43, and John Gingerich's article, 'Ignaz Schuppanzigh and Beethoven's Late Quartets', in *Musical Quarterly*, vol. 93, issue 3–4 (Oxford, 2010), pp. 450–513. The following translations of conversation book entries are by Elspeth Dusinberre.
9. Adelson, p. 224.
10. *Konversationshefte*, vol 7, p. 89.
11. *Briefwechsel*, vol. 6, no. 1940. Anderson, vol. 3, no. 1356.
12. Lockwood, p. 442.
13. *Konversationshefte*, vol. 7, p. 177.
14. Bäuerle, *Theaterzeitung* quoted in Thayer, ed. Forbes, vol. 2, p. 941.
15. *Konversationshefte*, vol. 7, p. 246.
16. *Konversationshefte*, vol. 7, p. 201.

17. *Konversationshefte*, vol. 8, p. 48.

18. *Konversationshefte*, vol. 7, p. 193.

19. *Konversationshefte*, vol. 10, p. 104.

20. *Konversationshefte*, vol. 8, pp. 52–3.

21. *Konversationshefte*, vol. 8, p. 281.

22. Albrecht, vol. 3, no. 405.

23. Anderson, vol. 3, no. 1405.

24. Albrecht, vol. 2, no. 333 and ft: the works mentioned were probably from among Opp. 109–111.

25. Albrecht, vol.3, no. 411.

26. Albrecht, vol. 2, no. 338.

27. Albrecht, vol. 3, nos. 370, 374 and 385.

28. Quoted in Thayer, ed. Forbes, vol. 2, p. 941.

29. Quoted in Thayer, ed. Forbes, vol. 2, p. 941.

5. Convalescence: Opus 132

1. In 1804 Franz II, the last Emperor of the Holy Roman Empire until it was dissolved in 1806, became Franz I, the first Emperor of Austria.

2. Ian Bradley, *Water Music: Making Music in the Spas of Europe and North America* (New York, 2010), pp. 56–9.

3. Bradley, p. 65, and H. C. Robbins Landon, *Haydn: The Years of 'The Creation'* (London, 1977), p. 497.

4. Quoted in Thayer, ed. Forbes, vol. 2, p. 888.

5. Maynard Solomon, *Beethoven Essays* (Cambridge, MA, 1988), p. 94.

6. *Briefwechsel*, vol. 2, no. 656. Anderson, vol. 1, no. 426.

7. *Briefwechsel*, vol. 4, no. 1493. Anderson, vol. 2, no. 1097.

8. *Briefwechsel*, vol. 6, no. 1967.

9. *Briefwechsel*, vol. 6, no. 1973. Anderson, vol. 3, no. 1373.

10. *Briefwechsel*, vol. 6, no. 1988. Anderson, vol. 3, no. 1386. Translation modified.

11. Sir George Smart, *Leaves from the Journals of Sir George Smart* (Cambridge, 1907/2014), pp. 108–9.

12. *Briefwechsel*, vol. 6, no. 1974.

13. *Briefwechsel*, vol. 6, no. 1980. Anderson, vol. 3, no. 1379.

14. *Briefwechsel*, vol.6, no. 1973. Anderson, vol.3, no. 1373.

15. Aldous Huxley, *Point Counter Point* (London: Chatto & Windus, 1928), reproduced by permission of The Random House Group Ltd, p. 560.

16. Huxley, p. 564.

17. Huxley, pp. 566–7.

18. Solomon, p. 249.

6. Alternative Endings: Opus 130

1. *Allgemeine musikalische Zeitung*, 28 (1826), quoted in Lockwood, p. 460.

2. The latter was transplanted from its original place as the music intended to follow the *Heiliger Dankgesang* in Opus 132.

3. Lockwood, p. 460 and p. 545 n. 36.

4. Lockwood, pp. 82–4.

5. Richard Kramer, '"Das Organische der Fuge": On the Autograph of Beethoven's Opus 59 no. 1', in Christoph Wolff (ed.), *The String Quartets of Haydn, Mozart and Beethoven: Studies of the Autograph Manuscripts* (Cambridge, MA, 1980), p. 229.

6. Kramer, pp. 237–41.

7. Cooper, p. 358.

8. See Chapter 1, n. 35.

9. Lenz, *Beethoven: Eine Kunststudie*, vol. 5, p. 218, quoted in Lockwood, p. 545, n. 35.

10. *Konversationshefte*, vol. 10, p. 104.

11. Lockwood, pp. 460–1.

12. Cooper, p. 364.

13. Alice M. Hanson, *Musical Life in Biedermeier Vienna* (Cambridge, 1985), pp. 43–4.

14. *King Lear* was in any case vulnerable to adaptation. Nathan Tate's 1681 version with its more cheerful ending was particularly popular, replacing Shakespeare's play in English-speaking performances well into the nineteenth century. Stanley Wells, *The Oxford Shakespeare: The History of King Lear* (Oxford, 2000), pp. 62–3.

15. Hanson, p. 46.

16. *Briefwechsel*, vol. 5, no. 1810.

17. Thayer, ed. Forbes, vol. 2, p. 910.

18. Mark Kanny, http://triblive.com/aande/music/6883563-74/quartet-beethoven-haydn#axzz3Vymd63do, last accessed 31 March 2015.

19. I am grateful to Matías Tarnopolsky, Director of CalPerformances, for his reflections on hearing ensembles play the two versions of Opus 130 during his years as a concert promoter.

20. Lockwood, p. 458.

21. Cooper, p. 372.

22. Lockwood, p. 479. Of the various translations offered, Lockwood's seems to me the most accurate.

23. *Briefwechsel*, vol. 6, no. 2224. Anderson, vol. 3, no. 1538.

24. Milan Kundera, *The Unbearable Lightness of Being*, translated by Michael Henry Heim (London: Faber and Faber, 1984), p. 189.

25. Laura Kathryn Bumpass, *Beethoven's Last Quartet*, Ph.D. diss. (University of Illinois, 1982).

26. *Briefwechsel*, vol. 6, no. 2236. Anderson, vol. 3, no. 1542. Translation modified.

27. *Briefwechsel*, vol. 6, no. 2234.

28. Gerhard von Breuning, *Memories of Beethoven: From the House of the Black-Robed Spaniards*, ed. Maynard Solomon, translated by Henry Mins and Maynard Solomon (Cambridge, 1992), p. 90.

29. *Briefwechsel*, vol. 6, no. 2285. Anderson, vol. 3, no. 1567.

30. Thayer, ed. Forbes, vol. 2, pp. 1101–3.

31. Thayer, ed. Forbes, vol. 2, p. 1057.

32. Margot Wetzstein (ed.), *Familie Beethoven im kurfürstlichen Bonn: Neuauflage nach den Aufzeichnungen des Bonner Bäckermeisters Gottfried Fischer* (Bonn, 2006), pp. 46–7, quoted in Jan Swafford, *Beethoven* (New York, 2014), pp. 22–3.

33. Cooper, p. 8.

34. H. C. Robbins Landon (ed.), *Beethoven, His Life, Work and World* (New York, 1992), p. 49.

35. Robbins Landon, *Beethoven*, p. 42.

36. Robbins Landon, *Beethoven*, p. 50.

Bibliography

Works cited

Adair, Sir Robert. *Historical Memoir of a Mission to the Court of Vienna in 1806*. London, 1844.

Adelson, Robert. 'Beethoven's String Quartet in E Flat Op. 127: A Study of the First Performances'. *Music and Letters*, vol. 79, no. 2. Oxford, 1998.

Albrecht, Theodore (ed.). *Letters to Beethoven and Other Correspondence*. 3 vols. Lincoln, NE, 1996.

Bashford, Christina. 'The string quartet and society'. In Robin Stowell (ed.), *The Cambridge Companion to the String Quartet*. Cambridge, 2003.

Beethoven, Ludwig van. *The Letters of Beethoven*. Translated and edited by Emily Anderson. 3 vols. London, 1961.

———. *Briefwechsel*. Edited by Sieghard Brandenburg. 7 vols. Munich 1996–8.

———. *Konversationshefte*. Edited by Karl-Heinz Köhler, Grita Herre and Dagmar Beck. 11 vols. Leipzig, 1972–2001.

Bradley, Ian. *Water Music: Making Music in the Spas of Europe and North America*. New York, 2010.

Breuning, Gerhard von. *Memories of Beethoven: From the House of the Black-Robed Spaniards*. Maynard Solomon (ed.). Translated by Henry Mins and Maynard Solomon. Cambridge, 1992.

Bumpass, Laura Kathryn. *Beethoven's Last Quartet*. Ph.D diss. University of Illinois, 1982.

Cooper, Barry. *Beethoven*. Oxford, 2000.

Coughlan, Robert. *Elizabeth and Catherine: Empresses of All the Russias*. New York, 1974.

De La Garde-Chambonas, August. *Anecdotal Recollections of the Congress of Vienna*. Translated by Maurice Fleury. London, 1902.

DeNora, Tia. *Beethoven and the Construction of Genius*. Berkeley, CA, 1995.

Gingerich, John. 'Ignaz Schuppanzigh and Beethoven's Late Quartets'. *Musical Quarterly*, vol. 93, issue 3–4. Oxford, 2010.

Hanson, Alice M. *Musical Life in Biedermeier Vienna*. Cambridge, 1985.

Heartz, Daniel. *Mozart, Haydn and Early Beethoven*. New York, 2009.

Huxley, Aldous. *Point Counter Point*. London, 1928.

Ingrao, Charles. *The Habsburg Monarchy*. Cambridge, 2000.

Kerman, Joseph. *The Beethoven Quartets*. New York, 1967.

————. 'Beethoven Quartet Audiences'. In Robert Winter and Robert Martin (eds), *The Beethoven Quartet Companion*. Berkeley, CA, 1994.

Kramer, Richard. '"Das Organische der Fuge": On the Autograph of Beethoven's Opus 59 no.1'. In Christoph Wolff (ed.), *The String Quartets of Haydn, Mozart and Beethoven: Studies of the Autograph Manuscripts*. Cambridge, MA, 1980.

Kundera, Milan. *The Unbearable Lightness of Being*. Translated by Michael Henry Heim. London, 1984.

Lockwood, Lewis. *Beethoven: The Music and the Life*. New York, 2003.

Owen, John. *Travels into Different Parts of Europe, in the Years 1791 and 1792*. 2 vols. London, 1796.

Razumovsky, Maria. *Die Razumovskys, Eine Familie am Zarenhof*. Cologne, 1998.

Reeve, Henry. *Journal of a Residence at Vienna and Berlin, in the Eventful Winter 1805–6*. London, 1877.

Riesbeck, Baron. *Travels Through Germany, in a Series of Letters*. Translated by Paul Henry Maty. London, 1787.

Robbins Landon, H. C. *Beethoven, His Life, Work and World*. New York, 1992.

————. *Haydn: The Years of 'The Creation'*. London, 1977.

Schindler, Anton. *Beethoven As I Knew Him: A Biography*. Edited by Donald W. MacArdle, translated by Constance S. Jolly. Chapel Hill, NC, 1966.

Senner, Wayne M., Robin Wallace and William Meredith (eds). *The Critical Reception of Beethoven's Compositions by his German Contemporaries*. 2 vols. Lincoln, NE, 1999.

Smart, Sir George. *Leaves from the Journals of Sir George Smart*. Cambridge, 1907/2014.

Solomon, Maynard. *Beethoven Essays*. Cambridge, MA, 1988.

Spiel, Hilde, ed. *The Congress of Vienna: An Eyewitness Account*. Translated by Richard H. Weber. Philadelphia, 1968.

Swafford, Jan. *Beethoven: Anguish and Triumph*. New York, 2014.

Thayer, Alexander Wheelock. *Thayer's Life of Beethoven*. Revised and edited by Elliot Forbes. 2 vols. Princeton, NJ, 1964.

Thürheim, Countess Lulu. *Mein Leben: Erinnerungen aus Österreichs grosser Welt 1788–1819*, 4 vols. Munich, 1913.

Tolstoy, Leo. *The Kreutzer Sonata*. Translated by Isai Kamen. New York, 2003.

Tyson, Alan. 'The Razumovsky Quartets: Some Aspects of the Sources'. In Alan Tyson (ed.), *Beethoven Studies 3*. New York, 1973.

Wegeler, Franz and Ferdinand Ries. *Beethoven Remembered*. Arlington, VA, 1987.

Wetzstein, Margot (ed.). *Familie Beethoven im kurfürstlichen Bonn: Neuauflage nach den Aufzeichnungen des Bonner Bäckermeisters Gottfried Fischer*. Bonn, 2006.

Winter, Robert. 'Quartets in Their First Century'. In Robert Winter and Robert Martin (eds), *The Beethoven Quartet Companion*. Berkeley, CA, 1994.

Further reading

Brion, Marcel. *Daily Life in the Vienna of Mozart and Schubert*. New York, 1962.

Burnham, Scott. *Beethoven Hero*. Princeton, NJ, 1995.

Burnham, Scott, and Michael P. Steinberg (eds). *Beethoven and His World*. Princeton, NJ, 2000.

Chua, Daniel. *'Galitzin' Quartets*. Princeton, NJ, 1995.

Cooper, Barry (ed.). *The Beethoven Compendium*. London, 1991.

Erickson, Raymond (ed.). *Schubert's Vienna*. New Haven, 1997.

Ferraguto, Mark. 'Russianness and Learned Style in the "Razu-movsky" String Quartets'. *Journal of the American Musicological Society*, vol. 67, no. 1. Berkeley, CA, 2014.

Glyde, Judith. 'Quarter of a Legend'. In *The Strad*, vol. 108, no. 1283. London 1997.

Kinderman, William. *Beethoven*. New York, 2009.

King, David. *Vienna 1814*. New York, 2008.

Mathew, Nicholas. *Political Beethoven*. Cambridge, 2013.

November, Nancy. *Beethoven's Theatrical Quartets: Opp. 59, 74 and 95*. Cambridge, 2013.

Rumph, Stephen. *Beethoven after Napoleon: Political Romanticism in the Late Works*. Berkeley, 2004.

Said, Edward W. *On Late Style: Music and Literature Against the Grain*. New York, 2006.

Solomon, Maynard. *Beethoven*. New York, 1998.

———. *Late Beethoven: Music, Thought, Imagination*. Berkeley, 2003.

Index